VIOLETS
THE HISTORY & CULTIVATION
OF SCENTED VIOLETS

VIOLETS

THE HISTORY & CULTIVATION
OF SCENTED VIOLETS

ROY E. COOMBS

B T BATSFORD

First Published 1981 by Croom Helm Ltd
Second edition 2003 by B T Batsford

© Text Roy E. Coombs 1981, 2003

The right of Roy E. Coombs to be identified as Author of this work has been asserted by him in accordance with the Copyright, Designs and Patents Act 1988.

Drawings and watercolour illustrations by Yvonne Matthews

© Volume B T Batsford 2003

ISBN 07134 8831 X

A CIP catalogue record for this book is available from the British Library.

Printed in China by South Sea International

for the publishers

B T Batsford
64 Brewery Road
London N7 9NY
England
www.batsford.com

A member of Chrysalis Books plc

INTRODUCTION

The violet's history over the centuries has been well documented but, surprisingly, the years of its greatest popularity have not been researched comprehensively. This book is not intended to be a complete work, as it would be pointless to restate material well set out elsewhere; but it will, I hope, act as a thorough guide to cultivated violets and their literature. So reading this book and then, if necessary, any of the older works described in the unique annotated bibliographical entries, should secure an understanding of the subject.

My aim has also been to shed some light onto areas of the subject which have been either ignored or inadequately researched in the past: the sections dealing with violet growing in comparatively modern times, the development of the various types of cultivated violet and the leading hybridizers and growers, have not been attempted before in this manner; and the lists of cultivars are more extensive and in greater detail than those published previously.

The Bibliography, for readers who wish to delve further into the subject, is also more extensive than any other compiled on the literature of the cultivated violets; indeed, most books contain few detailed indications of source material and the lack of a comprehensive subject bibliography was a serious handicap to me when beginning this research. I have also concentrated on passing, but important, references to violets in non-specialist works.

I must emphasize that I would recommend most of the books and articles listed for further reading, so it is because they are otherwise excellent that I have drawn attention to what I regard as being errors and discrepancies; but the most common fault is superficial coverage of the subject. It is regrettable that articles such as 'Russian Violets' by E. J. Perfect and books such as Nelson Coon's *Practical Violet Culture*, which do cover the intended subject authoritatively, are very rare.

Despite careful endeavour, I am sure that errors, discrepancies and omissions will be found in this present account and I should be grateful to learn of these so that they may be corrected in future editions.

INTRODUCTION TO THE SECOND EDITION

My aim in this second edition has been to give some account of violet growing since 1980 and also the results of historical research since then. The Bibliography has been considerably expanded partly with the help of the American Violet Society and likewise the descriptive lists of cultivars: that Society, working with the National Viola and Pansy Society of the UK, having been appointed the International Cultivar Registration Authority for the genus *Viola* in 2001.

Acknowledgements

Many people have helped with this project over the years. I am especially grateful to:

Mr C. D. Brickell, BSc (Hort.), VMH, Director of the Royal Horticultural Society's Garden, Wisley, England; Mr B. M. C. Ambrose, Information Officer of RHS Enterprises Ltd, Wisley, England; Miss Elspeth Napier, Editor, Royal Horticultural Society; Mr Nelson Coon, Massachusetts, USA; Mr Frank Groman, Oregon, USA; Mr A. G. L. Hellyer, MBE, VMH, AHRHS, FLS; Mr A. J. Huxley; Mr E. J. Perfect; Mrs P. Forsyth; Mr J. J. Leaman; Mr T. R. Pyne; Mr H. J. R. Rowe; Mrs E. White and Miss B. Zambra. Besides similarly acknowledging the general help and encouragement given by Mr P. G. Kettle and his relatives, I would also like to thank them for permitting me to include material from the extensive collection of unpublished notes left by the late Mr J. J. Kettle.

Some of that, as well as other material, now revised where necessary, first appeared in the *Journal of the Royal Horticultural Society* or in the Society's quarterly, *The Plantsman*. The annotated bibliographical entries for the works by Mrs Grace L. Zambra contain material first published in the *Dawlish Gazette*.

Finally, my thanks are due to the staffs of the Royal Horticultural Society's Lindley Library and various county and former municipal public libraries in the United Kingdom; also Mr J. T. Ashdown, Assistant to the Senior Horticultural Officer, Ministry of Agriculture, Fisheries and Food, as well as regional members of staff, in the south and west of England, of the Ministry's Agricultural Development and Advisory Service.

Roy E. Coombs

Acknowledgements for the second edition

Several of the people who helped with the former edition have again kindly helped with my research for this second edition and I would particularly like to thank E.J. Perfect whose original article in 1965 and subsequent correspondence not only encouraged my research but also my violet growing. My thanks additionally due to Yvonne, Clethra and Harry Matthews for their encouragement over the years backed by their experience caring for a UK national violet collection since 1984 and for the use of Yvonne and Clethra Matthews' paintings, drawings and photographs. Similarly thanks for the help and encouragement to Clive Groves and his late father, Charles Groves, and the use of photographs; to Jean Burrows for allowing me to participate in the excitement of the rediscovery of George Lee's violets; also the various owners of Lee's former nursery site for making me welcome; to Jean Canter for allowing the reproduction of possibly the sole surviving photograph of Clevedon violets from before World War I; to Jean Arnot and family members for allowing me to help in the revival of the Windward Violet Nurseries near Dawlish; to Peter Robinson not only for his assistance over the years but also in his current capacity as Registrar for Viola with John Snocken; to Mike Park for drawing my attention to the rare violet literature as had Mrs E. White previously; to Herb Saltford for information about the growing industry in New York State; to Norma Beredjiklian for permission to utilise International Violet Association material; to Barbara Corker for obtaining information concering Frederick Dillistone's nursery at Sturmer; the curators of the Henfield Museum for material concerning the Violet Nurseries at Henfield; to the Dawlish Museum and Jacqueline Sarsby for material relating to violet growing in South Devon and Tina Persaud of B T Batsford for advice during this revision.

Finally, a reference to my mother Elsie Coombs, who passed away a few months after the first edition was published. My mother gave vital help with the administration of my violet-growing enterprise at Winchester and then Honiton and also gave me the encouragement to become involved in horticulture.

Roy E. Coombs

CONTENTS

I

A HISTORY OF VIOLET CULTIVATION

The violet was one of the first flowering plants to be grown commercially: according to Theophrastus, they were being sold in the market at Athens *circa* 400BC, having been grown in specialist nurseries in Attica[1]. Sherbet, a favourite beverage in Asia Minor and the Middle East, contained violets, and Arab doctors are reputed to have prescribed oil extracted from violet seed as a remedy for the sting of the scorpion[2]. A manuscript Persian translation of a treatise on violet growing in Aramaic still exists[3]. The violet was referred to in Media and Persia as 'the prophet of the rose'[4]. Throughout the centuries, violets have been a favourite flower, written of by Horace and Juvenal as well as poets in recent times; they have been grown in monastery gardens and listed in old herbals. Gerard, writing in the sixteenth century, described violets as 'the greatest ornament, chiefest beauty and most excellent grace of gardens'.

Violet flowers were used to decorate and perfume rooms and the leaves were put in salads and other dishes. Wine used to be made from violets[5]. The flowers flavoured an artificial cream for sweets (candies) and other confectionery as well as being sold as 'crystallized violets' when candied by being coated with sugar and gum arabic.

Syrup of violets, a chemical indicator, which turned red when in contact with acids and green in the presence of alkalis, was obtained from violets, but litmus, which is used more widely for the same purpose in analysis today, is not distilled from violets as is sometimes stated[6], but from lichens. The French scientist Boullag, working in the early years of the nineteenth century, isolated the substance violine from violets and this has been described as a violent although uncertain emeto-cathartic[7].

Perfume could not be extracted from violet flowers until the nineteenth century. However, a few unrelated plants possessed a similar scent, notably a small number of orchids and the rhizomes of *Iris florentina* and some other iris species. The rhizomes of *I. florentina*, known as orris root, were the source of 'violet perfume'. The powdered root, sold as violet powder, was widely used as a perfume and as a base for tooth powder. Pieces of the dried root were given to teething babies to bite on. Besides being grown near Florence (Firenze), *I. florentina* was also produced at San Palo, a village near Parma, where for a time about 300 tons of the root were harvested annually, most being sent to the perfume manufacturers at Grasse in Provence[8]. Despite its popularity, orris perfume had critics, one of them being Alphonse Karr who described it as 'false' and 'acrid'[9].

The violet was sometimes grown on quite a large scale, as for instance in Provence where, in the mid-eighteenth century, olive plantations were uprooted and replaced with violets and other flowering plants[10]. But it was not until the end of the century, when the blossom and perfume became even more fashionable, that an increasing number of nurseries took up this crop, or were founded with violet cultivation in mind, to meet the demand, and thus participate in the profits that were often to be made. The violet was a favourite flower of Empress Josephine of France, first wife of Napoleon I. It was grown in the royal gardens at Malmaison and became a symbol of the House of Bonaparte. Napoleon made a promise to his supporters that he would escape from exile on Elba and return to France when the violets came into bloom again. Violets were planted on the grave of the Empress Josephine, and when Napoleon died, he was wearing a locket containing violet blossoms gathered from her grave before he began his final exile on St Helena. When the French monarchy was restored, the wearing of violets was banned and because of this, the former officers of Napoleon's army delighted in wearing them in their buttonholes. The violet became even more popular after Napoleon's nephew, Louis, seized power and ruled France as Napoleon III (1852). The violet was also a favourite flower of his wife, the Empress Eugénie, and following Napoleon III's death in 1873, during his exile in England, violet plants flourished on his mausoleum at Chislehurst in Kent. These events no doubt increased the popularity of the violet with the English. In France, despite the declaration of a republic, the flower remained very popular; for instance, in 1881 it was stated that about six million bunches of violets worth 577,000 francs were being handled by the Paris market each year.

Although the first attempts at violet growing near Paris (at Fresnes-les-Rungis) failed early in Napoleon I's reign, despite initial success, by the 1830s the industry was firmly established. This change was due in part to the outstanding cultivar 'La Violette des Quatre Saisons', introduced by Jean Chevillion of Fontenay-aux-Roses in 1835, which had a particularly long flowering season. Besides Fontenay, other increasingly important violet-growing centres in the Paris area were Bourg-la-Reine, Sceaux, Verrières, Belleville and Montreuil; at the last-named place, roses were also an important nursery crop, but such was the popularity of the violet that by 1889 only a few old rose bushes remained, with violets planted almost everywhere.

In England, the only large centre of violet cultivation had been near Stratford-upon-Avon, where in the late eighteenth and early nineteenth centuries, flowers were harvested for the manufacture of syrup of violets, the indicator used in chemical analysis. With the passing of the years, violets became grown increasingly for sale at the flower markets in Bristol, in the south-west, and London. At least one Bristol nurseryman, John Miller, was growing violets by 1826 when he was listing four hardy double cultivars in his catalogue, according to James C. House. During the 1840s and 1850s, following the introduction of the Russian violet, several nurseries were flourishing in and near Bristol and Bath. Around London, the orchards began to be underplanted with violets, and Cranford, Feltham, Hampton, Hounslow and Isleworth, all in the county of Middlesex, were important centres. At Cranford, 'The Czar', the first violet to receive an award from the Royal Horticultural Society (in 1865), was raised by F. J. Graham. In the issue of the *Gardeners Chronicle* dated 20 November 1880, a correspondent stated that 'all through the Middlesex market gardens violets are blooming freely now'.

However, violet growing near London was to decline, partly due to housing developments and partly due to the violets growing less well than formerly, possibly because of the increasing numbers of factories being set up in the towns of the Home Counties. James C. House mentioned (during the course of his lecture to Fellows of the Royal Horticultural Society) that in about 1887, Hampton was the chief violet-growing centre for the London markets: 'However by about 1902, the growers there were claiming that they could no longer grow violets.' A correspondent to the *Journal of Horticulture and Home Farmer*, perhaps after having witnessed yet another poor performance by his plants, wrote in April 1895: 'Twenty years ago the violet trade about London was a remarkable one, but we have rarely had good seasons for the flower since.' Feltham was still noted for its violets in 1899 according to W. E. Bear, writing in the *Journal of the Royal Agricultural Society of England*.

In the south of France, violets became a major crop, particularly after it was discovered how to extract the perfume from the flowers. La Valette-en-Var, near Toulon, became noted for its violets, while further west, violets were grown in the suburbs of Toulouse at Aucamville, Castelginest, Lalande, Launaguet, Saint-Alban and Saint-Jory. Magagnose and especially Hyères replaced La Valette-en-Var as the most important centres and the flowers were being sent to the perfume manufacturers at Grasse. In 1875, there were 1,200 acres of violets in the Hyères area alone and in 1900 that acreage had doubled. However, violet cultivation for this purpose had already started to decline: in 1893 two German scientists, V. Krüger and M. Tiemann, whilst analysing the orris root, discovered the chemical composition of its perfume, which was nearly identical to that of the violet. They patented their discovery, which they named Ionone after the Greek word for blue, ionon. Within a few years, the acreage under violets had been reduced by two-thirds[11] as ionone or methyl ionone became used as the base for many violet perfumes, although the finest contained a proportion of the natural violet extract. The chemical composition of the scent obtained from violet leaves, nonadeine, was closely imitated by methyl octane carbonate and W. A. Poucher considered that no violet perfume could be considered complete without the addition of this slightly earthy odour[12], presumably as 'it was thought that a bunch of violets embedded in the green leaves of the plant was far sweeter than that of the flowers by themselves'[13]. Only one-third of the remaining production of violets was for perfume, the rest being for cut flowers, particularly at Solliès-Pont in Le Var, and between Cannes and Vence for the local markets at Nice, Cannes and Antibes. The flowers were also sent to northern France where they competed, usually unsuccessfully, with those produced locally. Cut violets were exported from the south of France to Italy, Switzerland, Austria-Hungary, Germany and England.

The French violets were past their best by the time they arrived at the British markets, let alone the florists' shops. Nevertheless, home-produced violets continued for many years to be greatly outnumbered by those from France. The violet was the favourite flower of Queen Victoria, and also of Queen Alexandra whose interest was noted in the issue of the *Journal of Horticulture and Home Farmer* dated 3 April 1902:

> 'In the Royal Conservatory Gardens, Windsor Great Park, an especially fine specimen of double violet is being grown, which has gained the enthusiastic approval of The Queen. Her Majesty has said she has seen none finer and bunches are frequently forwarded to her.'

Public knowledge of this royal enthusiasm must have been a factor in the continuing expansion of violet growing in the United Kingdom. By the turn of the century, chrysanthemum shows often included classes for violets, examples being at Bristol, Frome and Torquay. Nurseries, often called violet farms, were founded in several counties in the south and south-west of England and in south-west Ireland. The cut flowers, as well as plants, were frequently sold direct to customers and even sent by mail. In addition, the existing large general nurseries devoted an increasing acreage to violets and the lists of cultivars in the catalogues became more and more extensive. The trends were very promising; James Udale's comment, published in 1910, that 'this charming and sweet flower is more extensively grown each year' could have been made with equal accuracy several years earlier or later[14].

The violet industry in the USA developed in a similar way to that in the UK, initially with violets of all types being grown in New England and in the Pacific coast states, but later an increasing emphasis was placed on the Parma cultivars. Examples of commercial violet holdings were those of Robert Armstrong at Mountain View, Santa Clara County, near San Francisco, where two acres of 'The Czar' and the Parma violet 'Marie Louise' were being grown in 1895, and of a Mr Bonnell, further north, who was growing 8,000 plants of 'Princesse de Galles' and 2,000 'Marie Louise'. Violet nurseries were to be found near most of the large towns and cities in both the eastern and western coastal states. George Saltford pioneered violet growing at Rhinebeck-on-Hudson in about 1890. This area had good rail connections with New York City, which ensured that the flowers would reach the markets quickly; another advantage was that vast quantities of manure could be obtained from the stables in New York for spreading on the land. Within 15 years Rhinebeck and the surrounding district had become the major production area for violets in the entire country. The New York Botanic Gardens held exhibitions of violets; the flower market in that city handled 1.5 million violet flowers each day in the season and thousands of bunches were sold in the streets daily. Violets were just as popular in other American cities, too. Due to difficulties caused by the intensive glasshouse cultivation and also to changing fashion, the Parmas were largely replaced by the giant singles, with firstly 'California' becoming widely grown, and later tens of thousands of plants of 'Princesse de Galles' were grown. Cliftonville, Massachusetts, was the location of what was claimed to be the largest nursery in the world devoted to violet cultivation and its output was between three and four million flowers annually.

In Ireland, violet growing was attracting attention; some of the first farms were often run as paying hobbies by members of the titled families, partly as a means of alleviating unemployment. Violets were grown in quantity at Adare, Co. Limerick, and Ennis, Co. Clare, but it was in Co. Cork, particularly in the area around Skibereen, that most of the Irish violets were grown:

> 'Of late years in the county of Cork, the culture of violets is largely carried on, and in such far places violet farms of three or four acres produce very considerable incomes to the fair and enterprising farmer.'[15]

There is a little evidence to suggest that commercial violet growing in that extreme south-western county had been attempted earlier in the nineteenth century, but the first successful grower was Mrs Egerton Coghill of Glen Barrahane, Castletownshend. Mrs Coghill sought to encourage the establishment of more violet farms, and a co-operative, Castlehaven Garden Industries, was formed by local horticulturists. W. Miles of Ballydehob, a few miles west of Skibereen, was one of the most important growers, and it was the success, which he enjoyed in the years immediately prior to World War I that probably influenced some of the pioneer growers in the south-west of England where the climate is similar to that of Co. Cork.

Violets grown commercially in Devonshire only met the local demand until 1891 when two brothers named Westcott, who grew violets at Cockwood near

Starcross, sent a few bunches by train to London and found that demand in the capital (and therefore returns) far exceeded those in Devon[16]. Other pioneer growers were J. Heath and R. W. Beachey at Kingskerswell between Torquay and Newton Abbot. The first violet farm was established at Dawlish in 1916 and from then onwards several holdings sprang up in the Teignmouth, Holcombe, Dawlish, Starcross and Kenton area. By 1926 the numbers of British violets reaching the markets at last equalled those imported from France and the steady expansion continued until 1930, helped by the government imposing a tariff on imported flowers. A 'boom' in violet growing then took place with a 500 per cent increase in acreage in the Dawlish area by 1936.

The proprietor of a three-acre violet farm at Holcombe made £1,300 during the 1935–36 flowering season, and this has been referred to frequently since that time; however, to put it into perspective, the same grower had made only £400 in the previous flowering season when east winds blew without abating for three months and severely reduced the yield of blooms[17]. Mr and Mrs George Zambra's Windward Violet Nurseries was perhaps the most enterprising of the new businesses; founded in 1922, the Nurseries exhibited at the Daily Mail Ideal Home Exhibition in London on several occasions, as well as at the Royal Horticultural Society's shows. This marked increase in violet cultivation in the Dawlish area was rather surprising as it coincided with a period of severe aphis infestation there, which might have been expected to deter intending growers (see Chapter 9).

Although the spread of London took much of the land that had been used for violet growing, cultivation under glass in Middlesex continued until well after the end of World War II. These plants were still grown commercially elsewhere in south-east England, for example at Sturmer on the borders of Suffolk and Essex where the Dillistone family, who had been violet growers for more than 200 years, continued trading until the 1940s, and The Violet Nurseries, Henfield, Sussex, founded by the 'Misses Allen-Brown' continued until the early 1950s. In south Dorset and neighbouring parts of south-west Hampshire, violet growing became increasingly important at Corfe Mullen, Wimborne, Ferndown, Broadstone and Bransgore. The most famous business in this area was J. J. Kettle's Violet Farm at Corfe Mullen, founded in 1905, which soon covered several acres and included large glasshouses; it was from there that the sensational award-winning, semi-double, giant-flowered cultivars were introduced. General nurseries in southern England still offering a wide range of violets included those of Bunyards Royal Nurseries at Maidstone, Kent, and the Royal Nurseries at Slough, Buckinghamshire, founded by Charles Turner. Further west, Blackmore and Langdon at Twerton-on-Avon near Bath and Isaac House and Son of Westbury-on-Trym, near Bristol, continued the violet-growing tradition in one of its original centres.

Frederick E. Dillistone noted in 1927 that the violet was still being held in favour by the Royal Family:

'On the departure recently of the Duke and Duchess of York to Australia, every photograph and film depicting the Duchess's vivacity and charm of manner, showed her dress resplendent with violets.'[18]

This royal partiality, as mentioned previously, must have helped strengthen the violet's position with the flower-buying public. And in 1930, H. H. Warner commented in his account:

'When visiting London in January, to hear the carillon of bells erected in Hyde Park before going to New Zealand as a war memorial, [I saw] flower sellers ... standing at the street corners with large baskets piled high with bunches of fragrant, deep purple single violets, and also the mauvedouble ones.'[19]

C. H. Cook, when writing in 1935 about the royal gardens at Windsor, mentioned that Queen Mary appeared to favour the carnation, closely followed by the rose, daffodil and violet[20].

Violet growing in the USA had reached its zenith in the early 1900s when it was third in commercial importance, surpassed only by the rose and the carnation. The intensive glasshouse cultivation that had first led to difficulties with the Parmas later affected the giant singles, which had tended to replace them. To overcome this, hybrids were developed between the giant singles and unscented large-flowered native species. These hybrids almost totally lacked perfume but had an increased resistance to pest and disease attacks. 'Governor Herrick' was one of the first of these introductions and it also achieved popularity with British growers after being imported just prior to the outbreak of World War I.

In France and Germany, other than for perfume manufacture, violet growing had lost much of its importance and in the UK, too, there was a steady decline from World War II onwards, so much so that the Rosewarne Experimental Horticultural Station near Camborne in Cornwall, which had been set up to assist local growers of horticultural crops, abandoned its trials of various violet cultivars in the 1960s.

However, plantations of West Country violets were to the enthusiast as impressive as their often scenic surroundings:

'In Devon one of the biggest centres of the industry is at Holcombe, a small village between Dawlish and Teignmouth ... Just now, at the height of the season, every little farmhouse in the area ... is packed with flowers. The ladies of the house are busy all day sorting, tying-up and packing. Men bring more in continually.'[21]

Also in the 1930s, *The King's England* volume on the subject of Cornwall contained this reference to the five inhabited Isles of Scilly, 30 miles from Land's End:

'They are like gardens of indescribable beauty when the daffodils and violets and anemones are out. They bloom everywhere, the flowers come to London from sheltered valleys and the ledges of cliffs dipping into the sea. They are picked, packed, and despatched the same day, and arrive fresh daily after a sea voyage and a journey of 300 miles on a flower express train.'[22]

Twenty-five years later, in 1961, Derek Tangye described the crop in the Lamorna valley of south-west Cornwall:

'In winter … the air is sweet with the scent of the violet plants which climb up the hillsides in neat rows, and as you walk along you meet a picker, a basket of violets or anemones in hand, taking them home to bunch.'[23]

The *Red Guide to Devon*, published in 1969, also includes a note about violet growing in the county:

'On the sunny hillsides violets bloom from September till mid April and flower-growing – particularly the fragrant 'Princess of Wales' violet, is one of the chief industries of Dawlish. Boxes of flowers are sent to all parts of Britain and to the Continent.'[24]

Violets are still grown at Dawlish. They were also grown in the Torridge valley of north Devon in quite recent years but at Topsham on the eastern bank of the Exe estuary, where they were grown at George Pyne's Denver Nurseries, later of raspberry fame, they are but a memory. The Falmouth area of Cornwall, especially Constantine, Feock and Mylor, has been noted for its violets, also Lelant, Hayle, Paul and St Buryan, besides Lamorna already mentioned.

The demand for violets has increased from the late 1960s onwards, and acreages under the crop should expand. Another consequence may be that existing cultivars will become plentiful and new cultivars will be raised and introduced. Previous expansions of violet growing have coincided with times of high unemployment; whether this will prove to be the case in present conditions is dependent to a great extent on a willingness of existing growers and enthusiasts to work together.

NOTES

1. Gabriel Tergit, *Flowers Through the Ages* (Wolff, 1961).

2. Edward Hyams, *The Gardener's Bedside Book* (Faber, 1968).

3. Alice M. Coats, *Flowers and Their Histories* (Hulton Press, 1956).

4. Gabriel Tergit, *Flowers Through the Ages* op cit.

5. Coats, *Flowers and Their Histories*.

6. G. Bazin, *A Gallery of Flowers* (Thames and Hudson, 1960).

7. Edward Hyams, *The Gardener's Bedside Book* op cit.

8. Gabriel Tergit, *Flowers Through the Ages* op cit.

9. Alphonse Karr, *A Tour Round My Garden* (Routledge, 1855).

10. Gabriel Tergit, *Flowers Through the Ages* op cit.

11. Gabriel Tergit, op cit.

12. W. A. Poucher, *Perfumes, Cosmetics and Soap* (Chapman and Hall), 1959.

13. Ernest J. Parry, *Cyclopaedia of Perfumery*: a Handbook (J. & A. Churchill, 1925).

14. James Udale, *Gardening for All* (Simpkins, 1910).

15. F. C. Hayes, *A Handy Book of Horticulture* (Murray, 1901).

16. Ronald Webber, *Market Gardening* (David and Charles, 1972).

17. Grace L. Zambra, *Violets for Garden and Market* (W.H. & L. Collingridge, 1938).

18. Frederick E. Dillistone, 'The Cult of the Violet', *Gardening Illustrated* 30 April 1927.

19. H. H. Warner, 'Violets in Many Lands and Ages', *Gardening Illustrated* 5 July 1930.

20. C. H. Cook, 'The Gardens of Their Majesties The King and Queen at Windsor', *Journal of the Royal Horticultural Society* (May 1935).

21. *Express and Echo* (6 February 1936).

22. Arthur Mee (ed.), *Cornwall* (Hodder and Stoughton, 1937).

23. Derek Tangye, *A Gull on the Roof* (Michael Joseph, 1961).

24. *Red Guide to Devon* (Ward Lock, 1969).

Violet history since 1980

I wrote about the risk of violet cultivars becoming extinct in an article, 'Vanishing Violets', published in *Amateur Gardening* in 1968. The trend steadily continued with lists of cultivars being rationalized and nurseries ceasing to trade, and this did not just involve violets but also many other cultivated plants.

The Hardy Plant Society produced a plant finder publication, which not only helped find plants but also highlighted the cultivars listed by very few nurseries and those not stocked by any nursery. I wrote two articles for a gardening periodical on the general threat in 1980 and gave specific examples of plants at risk including a few violets. I had already produced lists of desirable cultivars of various species as part of an exercise being supervised by A. G. L. Hellyer.

The National Council for the Conservation of Plants and Gardens was set up and the formation of county branches was encouraged. Another aspect of the work of the NCCPG was the setting up of National Collections of specific plants. I was involved in correspondence with the University of Leicester when they were considering becoming the National Collection Holder for Viola. The University decided not to take on violets and Yvonne Matthews took on this task and still maintains one of the two National Collections of violets in the UK. National Collection schemes have been organized in other countries, too.

Back in 1964 I had been informed that the Windward Violet Nurseries site was going to be developed. Years later I saw fairly new houses from the main road and wrongly believed these had been built on the nursery. Later still when researching for the first edition of this book, I visited J. J. Leaman who largely specialized in violets. During one of those visits I was told that he had just been contacted by a resident with violets of many colours in her garden. The 'garden' turned out to be the original Windward site, which had not been developed after all. Over the next few years the owners revived the nurseries. When a decision was taken to cease trading, plants were widely distributed to other nurseries including C. W. Groves and Son of Bridport and West Winds Nursery, Hereford, as well as to the National Collection.

History had repeated itself: I had maintained a large collection of violets in Winchester following the demise of Windward in 1964 and then the demise of The Violet Farm, Corfe Mullen in 1968, followed shortly after by Maurice Pritchard's Riverslea Nurseries at Christchurch. These violets were sold all over the country and different cultivars acquired. An increasingly wide range was maintained at Winchester until 1974, with a duplicate collection being donated to the RHS Garden at Wisley. The revived Windward nurseries continued the process and since the nurseries closed down for the second time, Groves have built up a larger and larger collection of violets.

During 1986 Jean Burrows, who had found many different violets growing on the slopes of Tickenham Hill near Clevedon, was advised to contact me. Ironically, a local newspaper had stated only some three years before that Clevedon violets, once so famous, had vanished. The survival of those violets was even more remarkable; the Windward violets had survived untended for about 12 years but those at Clevedon had existed for many more years than that, probably at least 50, since the nursery was subdivided, but in all the new gardens the violets continued to flourish. The rediscovered Lee violets (bred by George Lee) were added to the National Collection and, despite an initial setback, have also been widely distributed.

In addition to the redistribution of the Lee violets, the violet world also had the opportunity to acquire the Wylde Green Cottage Violets raised in New Zealand by Kerry Carman; as with the Lee violets the exercise was not without its setbacks: cultivars are available though not so easily as one might wish.

The 1990s have been a time of close contact between violet growers, both amateur and professional, in various parts of the world. I had contacts in the USA, the Netherlands and Argentina; and from my former Honiton nursery I had established contact with a violet nursery in France and my Parma violets and other plants had been successfully approved for export. Yvonne Matthews, as a National Collection Holder, and C. W. Groves and Son of Bridport have developed far more extensive links at home and abroad, resulting in the frequent interchange of violet plants. Cultivars thus believed lost here are now being supplied from growers abroad and vice versa, where legally permissible.

The Hardy Plant Society established a Viola Group, which published a Newsletter that ran to five issues. An article in an American magazine led to the formation of the North American Violet Fanciers Association, which soon evolved into the International Violet Association. It was a great honour to be invited to be the Association's first President but I would emphasize that the hard work in developing the association was done by others. The links between growers were further enhanced by the launch of the Association's Newsletter (and later Journal for the genus *Viola*) entitled *Sweet Times*.

The Association held a conference or symposium most years, with venues as varied as San Francisco, Dawlish and Toulouse. All these activities strengthened the links and achieved publicity for the Association and for the violet. Following the successful Toulouse Conference, it was decided to separate the Association into two. One part, based in the USA, became the American Violet Society and publishes newsletters and a gazette on the internet. The AVS has also been approved as the host for the international name list of violet cultivars. The other part, based mainly in Europe, soon developed links with The Violet Society, which was already publishing a journal on the internet. One of the differences is that the American Violet Society has an annual membership subscription (in the same way as most other societies and associations) and parts of its website are restricted to members only, whereas The Violet Society has no membership subscription and its website is available to all at the time of writing.

The Violet Society was also involved in a symposium/visit to the north of Italy sponsored by the Devon Violet Nursery. This venue was chosen, like those of the IVA, because of a considerable tradition of violet growing.

The development of the Devon Violet Nursery has to be one of the events of this period; the former Christianson-owned nursery specialized in its last years in the scentless cultivar 'Governor Herrick', but the new owners quickly built up a collection of violets that was deemed suitable by the NCCPG to be a second National Collection in this country. Mrs Joan Yardley's efforts in promoting the nursery, violets and the Europe-based part of the old association, of which she was President, are almost legendary.

However, the continuing commitment of Yvonne Matthews, Clive Groves and his family, and growers overseas such as Rob Peace in Victoria, Australia (the National Collection Holder there) and John Whittlesey (a former IVA President) in California, in addition to the memberships of the two societies as well as more localized societies in France and Japan, has ensured that the cultivation of scented violets is on a much sounder footing than in 1980.

2

SCENTED SINGLE VIOLETS

(HARDY)

Viola odorata is a native plant of many European countries. The flowers are usually violet in colour, but the white form *alba* is quite common and in some areas, such as part of Hampshire, in England, outnumbers the original type. Other mutations are sometimes found, for instance, the subsequently named 'Norah Church' with lilac flowers, which was collected growing in the wild and introduced in the 1920s. Most of the various colour forms being grown in gardens in Tudor times would have originated in the same way, although of course some may have appeared in gardens. Until the nineteenth century, few new forms were introduced, but then the greatly increased interest resulted in new violets being found and they multiplied quickly.

The Russian violet was introduced in this country before 1830 as an earlier and hardier violet. *Viola suavis*, with paler flowers than the Russian violet, may also have reached here from Russia at about the same time. Improved forms of the Russian violet such as 'Russian Superb' and 'The Giant', as well as 'Devoniensis', which was probably evolved from *V. suavis*, became the leading sorts grown for cut-flower production. In France 'La Violette des Quatre Saisons' (introduced by Jean Chevillion of Fontenay-aux-Roses in 1835) and its descendants, with a much longer flowering season, became the leading commercial sorts.

'The Czar', an improved Russian seedling, was raised in 1863 by F. J. Graham of Cranford, Middlesex, England, and received the Royal Horticultural Society's First Class Certificate two years later. This violet was almost true purple in colour and probably slightly larger than the Russian violets. In France a violet cultivar, 'Wilson', was imported from Algeria and possibly also from Turkey in 1869. It had paler flowers than those already growing in France, but they were also larger and it immediately found favour in Provence. This cultivar, quite possibly a form of *Viola suavis*, was crossed with 'The Czar' by Armand Millet of Bourg-la-Reine near Paris and a succession of seedlings was introduced that in the main differed greatly from existing violets by way of larger size, improved shape and wider colour range. The giant scented cultivars such as 'Princesse de Galles' and 'Souvenir de Ma Fille' were among the seedlings raised by the Millet family over many years (see Chapter 7).

George Lee of Clevedon, Somerset steadily developed the range of Russian violets by crossing 'The Czar' with other popular cultivars, his first important introduction being 'Victoria Regina', the result of a cross between 'The Czar' and 'Devoniensis' in 1873 (see Chapter 7). Other French growers, besides Armand Millet, had similar if much more limited successes, for instance 'Rubra' raised by L. Paillet of Châtenay-les-Sceaux and 'Amiral Avellan' from L. Lille of Lyon. However, Millet's seedlings were in a class apart, as the rounded petal so common today was originated by him with cultivars such as 'Gloire de Bourg-la-Reine' in 1879.

In Provence, a form of 'The Czar', named 'Czar Bleu' (later renamed 'Reine Victoria'), began to replace 'Wilson' and 'The Czar' in the principal area around Hyères. A seedling of it that appeared in the gardens of the Baronne Alice de Rothschild was named after her and although this flower was never widely grown for perfume manufacture, it was grown for cut flowers and also became an important early-flowering cultivar in Britain. 'Luxonne', one of several cultivars obtained by crossing 'The Czar' and 'Wilson', became with its seedlings the leading sort used by growers supplying the perfume industry. 'Princesse de Galles' and similar cultivars were never grown a great deal in Provence except for sending to the markets of northern France and Switzerland, but with its long thick stems, and almost circular large flowers and fine leaves, it became widely planted in the north of France and in Britain. Violets were also grown in other countries from where allegedly new cultivars of the same type appeared: 'Boston' and 'California' (USA), 'Askania' and 'Kaiser Wilhelm II' (Germany), and 'Italia' and 'Primavera' (Italy). A writer in *Gardeners Chronicle* summed up the position:

> 'Vast changes in the last half dozen years have added 3 to 4 inches [7.5 to 10 cm] to the stems and petals 50% larger have added immensely to the cutting value [however] some have maintained that the fragrance of 'California' and 'Princess of Wales' is not so pronounced as the older varieties, others that the size is a drawback.'

The colour range was being extended continually, particularly among the smaller flowered violets – 'John Raddenbury', 'Mignonette' and 'St Helena' (pale blues); 'Mme Armandine Pagès' and 'Rosea Delicatissima' (pale pinks); 'Principessa di Summunte' (pale blue on white ground); and the probably distinct species *Viola vilmorini* or *V. sulfurea*, with apricot and cream scentless flowers, which was hailed as a yellow sweet violet. Later, in the 1920s, 'Coeur d'Alsace' with unique rosy-salmon flowers became very popular and in Britain a cultivar with purple markings on a white ground appeared under a variety of names such as 'Mrs R. Barton', 'Alassio' and 'Constance Apthorp'. 'Tina Whitaker', which had been found in Sicily, was also introduced about this time;

its flowers were elongated and were probably the largest of any scented violet. 'Mrs F. B. Dwight', probably selected from 'Princesse de Galles', was introduced just prior to World War II and was grown quite extensively in Cornwall for some years. 'Windward' with flowers of a rosy crimson shade and 'Red Queen', described as a form of 'Coeur d'Alsace', with magenta flowers, were the only cultivars of more recent introduction to become firmly established by 1980. The fascinatingly coloured 'Opéra', described as being new even in the final list issued by the Windward Violet Nurseries in the early 1960s, had in fact been introduced in c.1930.

In terms of numbers and of colours, the range of single-flowered violet cultivars readily available in the UK has increased considerably since 1980. New seedlings have been introduced and cultivars thought possibly extinct have been rediscovered, sometimes overseas.

Early this century cultivars resulting from crosses between scented violets and unscented native species such as *Viola sororia* were introduced in the USA, where they were considered to be easier to grow under the exceptionally intensive commercial conditions. 'Governor Herrick' and its seedling 'Frey's Fragrant' were among the first to be introduced; the latter has been described as not living up to its name, and while the former was introduced by Blackmore and Langdon as very sweetly scented, it is doubtful whether the flowers now carry any perfume at all. An additional disadvantage is that the stems and foliage are brittle and so are easily damaged, a characteristic inherited from the American species. Runners are not produced, another similarity to the American species, but there are two important differences: the foliage does not die down in winter and flowers are produced in the same season as scented violets instead of in summer like the species.

Despite the faults of 'Governor Herrick', many violet farmers thought that its advantages made its cultivation worthwhile and it became the most widely grown violet in Britain. The blame for the belief that violets were losing their scent should indeed rest with 'Governor Herrick' and sales of both plants and flowers of scented cultivars may well have been adversely affected. However, the introduction of more effective acaracides has not resulted in a large increase in the acreage of scented violets, and in any case cultivars such as 'California' were already resistant to red spider mite. It is quite probable that the elimination of the chore of derunnering during the summer, and the simple and speedy method of propagation by division, had as much to do with the success of 'Governor Herrick' as did its almost total immunity to infestation by red spider mites.

However, every year 'Bournemouth Gem' flowers seem to form an increasing proportion of the total. There is some confusion regarding the name of this comparatively new (for a violet) cultivar, as both 'Bournemouth Blue' and 'Bournemouth Gem' have been used. H. R. Jones and Son of Corfe Mullen included both 'Bournemouth Blue' and 'Governor Herrick' in their price list. The Windward Violet Nurseries, in their last years of trading, considered some stocks of 'Bournemouth Blue', 'Bournemouth Gem' and 'Mrs Pinchurst' identical to their own 'Pamela Zambra', despite Grace Zambra referring to these as distinct cultivars in the second edition of *Violets for Garden and Market* – incorrect labelling has clearly been a problem for many years. 'Governor Herrick' also appeared in the Windward lists.

These facts need not conflict if one assumes that a stock of 'Pamela Zambra' became incorrectly labelled 'Bournemouth Blue'. Without any doubt, 'Bournemouth Gem' is distinct from 'Governor Herrick', 'Mrs Pinchurst' and 'Pamela Zambra' as it does have a slight violet perfume which is retained by the flowers for a few days after picking, as opposed to the scentless 'Governor Herrick', and 'Pamela Zambra' which loses its scent an hour or so after picking. There are other differences besides scent and no mention was made in the Rosewarne Experimental Horticultural Station's reports of any suspicion of synonymy, despite stocks of all three cultivars being grown there.

Derek Tangye mentioned that the foliage of 'Bournemouth Gem' perfumed the meadows even before the flowers appeared[1] and that cultivar has been regarded by the Ministry of Agriculture as a selection from 'Governor Herrick'; indeed, if the latter were originally scented, a reversion may have occurred to the original type, as regards this property at least, as the plants certainly look very similar. 'Mrs Pinchurst' has flowers of a slightly more purple colour, and foliage which is distinct from 'Governor Herrick' and 'Bournemouth Gem', although the habit is the same. 'Pamela Zambra' is similar in colour to 'Mrs Pinchurst'; its foliage and habit show the same general characteristics but in detail they are quite different. One of the main differences is that quite long 'runners' are produced by 'Pamela Zambra' plants although these are much thicker stemmed than those of *V. odorata* cultivars.

Mrs Zambra has recorded that 'Pamela Zambra' was a seedling of Armand Millet's 'Explorateur Dybowski' and as it was a great improvement, she discarded the parent cultivar. This does seem to have been unfortunate as not only did 'Explorateur Dybowski' have flowers of an unusual metallic violet colour, but it was one of the very few violets highly resistant to red spider mite and, while Mrs Zambra described it as scentless, its raiser described it as scented. Also, while we know that 'Explorateur Dybowski' was capable of producing seed, 'Pamela Zambra' does not appear to be, and so, in the one direction at least, the chance of crossing with the 'Governor Herrick' type cultivars has been lost.

I wrote in 1980 that it would have been interesting to have tried crossing 'Explorateur Dybowski' with other *V. odorata* cultivars, perhaps a pink one for example. It is possible that such an opportunity may again be available soon, as it is believed that 'Explorateur Dybowski' has been rediscovered in Queensland, Australia.

The range of colour of these violets is very restricted, even allowing for 'Frey's Fragrant', not offered for sale in this country, and which must rank as the most tiresomely named cultivar, as, after every mention of it, one has to point out that it is unscented (but could 'Frey's Fragrant', 'Governor Herrick' and even 'Explorateur Dybowski', have lost their perfume over the years? A thought that now has to be qualified as the supposed Queensland 'Explorateur Dybowski' flowers are recorded as being slightly fragrant). The only hybridizer working with these violets in fairly recent years had been Mrs Edith Pawla of the Pawla Violet Farm, Santa Cruz, California. The cultivars raised there mainly had large flowers on long stems. 'Royal Robe' was one of the most commonly listed of these in the USA. It had reached the Windward Violet Nurseries by the early 1980s from Cornwall and it is now quite widely listed.

Besides crossing with *V. odorata* cultivars, the use of the American Giant Violets could perhaps yield white and magenta as well as true violet seedlings. It might be necessary to cloche the American Giants to ensure simultaneous flowering. Also the Type 2 species (*priceana*) does yield seedlings of various types, and winter flowering might be introduced into its progeny. It should be remembered that the perfume when present among the hybrids is only slight, so that too much 'blood' of unscented species could dilute it almost to non-existence. It is perhaps surprising that little or no research work has been done with these violets in recent years, as it would seem that it is this class and the Parma violets that hold the greatest promise for cut-flower growers as labour becomes increasingly expensive. Also, these violets make fine subjects for planting towards the front of herbaceous borders.

Descriptive lists of cultivars of the various types of violets appeared in the first edition of this book in 1981. I made no claim that those lists were complete but a wide range of books, periodicals and nursery catalogues had been consulted during compilation. The American Violet Society, during 2001, was appointed International Cultivar Registration Authority for the genus *Viola*. The Society is thus committed to compile and maintain an International Register of *Viola* cultivars. The Register is in preparation and has clearly benefited from the availability of my cultivar lists published in the first edition of this book. The Society in return has provided me with information it has been collecting, to help update the following lists.

The list of single-flowered cultivars of *Viola odorata* and those of other types of violets included in this guide have been compiled using a wide range of books, periodicals and nursery catalogues for reference, but no claim is made that they are complete.

Many of the cultivars listed may have been extinct for a long time but are of use in tracing the development of the scented violet.

Unfortunately many of the older nursery catalogues do not seem to have been preserved. For instance, I had only found three editions of the Windward Violet Nurseries' lists but the total now found is at least five; the last list issued by The Violet Farm, Corfe Mullen in the 1960s has been supplemented by one from *c*.1930 and, similarly with Dillistones of Sturmer, lists discovered from 1869–70 and 1870–71 have also been supplemented by one from *c*.1930.

THE CULTIVARS

The entry for each cultivar comprises the following information when known: name of cultivar; name of raiser; country of origin (if not the United Kingdom); approximate year of introduction or year in which the earliest mention of the cultivar has been traced; the parents of the cultivar; awards received and a description of the cultivar. Yvonne Matthews, who has been a national violet collection holder since soon after the start of the National Council for the Conservation of Plants and Gardens national collections scheme, has provided Royal Horticultural Society Colour Chart references where these are available. Inevitably some cultivar names lack any detail.

In general, the entries for cultivars raised by George Lee and Armand Millet are very short, but fuller descriptions will be found in Chapter 7. Finally, names of probable synonyms are included and these are also cross indexed within the alphabetical sequence.

The following abbreviations have been used: AM Award of Merit; CM Certificate of Merit; FCC First Class Certificate; FCHS Central Horticultural Society (of France); FNHS The National Horticultural Society (of France); RHS Royal Horticultural Society; MRCF Ministry Recommended Cut Flower where the cultivar was included in the Ministry of Agriculture series of advisory leaflets on Violets.

CULTIVARS OF SCENTED SINGLE VIOLETS (HARDY)

'Abonnen Neveu' (France, 1890; 'Luxonne' seedling). Large flowered blue.

'Ada Segre' (Nathalie Casbas, France, *c*.2000). Very large blue flowers.

'Admiral Avellan', see 'Amiral Avellan'.

'Adriana' Free-flowering cultivar exhibited by Miss A. Balmer, Clapper Knap, Porlock Weir, Somerset, at a meeting of the RHS on 13 February 1894.

'Alassio' Was regarded in the 1920s and 1930s as the largest single white violet and it appeared in the same lists as 'Mrs R. Barton', to which cultivar it was later thought to be synonymous even though the latter is not a (pure) white violet.

'Alexandra' (Australia). Coral pink. See also 'Princess Alexandra'.

'Alice' (Australia). Medium-sized lilac flowers shaded with grey. Intense perfume.

'**American Red Beauty**' (USA). Luminous red flowers, velvety petals. Unusual.

'**Amethyst**' (Australia). No description available.

'**Amethyst Queen**' (Australia). No description available.

'**Amiral Avellan**' (Léonard Lille, Lyon, France, 1893). AM, RHS 1897. Opening flower buds are deeper in colour than 'Princess Alexandra'. Reddish-purple 81A-80A but fades leaving deeper veining. Nearer to red under glass. Very free-flowering. Very hardy and dependable. Invasive: if this cultivar fails, other single-flowered cultivars in the same conditions are unlikely to succeed. Strong perfume. Also listed as 'Admiral Avellan'. MRCF.

'**Amiral de Breton**', see 'Princess Alexandra'.

'**Annie**' (C. W. Groves & Son, Bridport, Dorset, 2001). Small to medium-sized flowers of carmine, deeper at upper centre of middle lower petal. Slightly more purple than 'Perle Rose' and a much longer flowering season.

'**Argentiflora**' (George Lee, Clevedon, Somerset, 1879). Silvery-mauve 85C. Long flowering season. Also listed as 'Argentacflora'.

'**Askania**' (Germany, 1908). CM, Society for the Development of Horticulture in the Kingdom of Prussia; CM, Union of German Horticulturists. Giant-flowered deep violet blue 86A with somewhat pointed petals. Long stems. Very free flowering. Most growers have commented favourably on this really outstanding cultivar. MRCF.

'**Aubéreinne**', see 'Souvenir de Jules Josse'.

'**Aurantiaca**', see 'Sulfurea'.

'**Australian Red**'. Has been grown in the USA. No description available.

'**Baby Rose**' (McLeod, NSW, Australia, 1993; 'Rosea' x 'Amiral Avellan'). Small flowers of a deep rich rose pink. Very fragrant.

'**Barensteinii**' (1886). Bluish purple. Possibly synonymous with 'Barenstein's Saemling' (Otto Mann, Germany, c.1884). Medium-sized flowers and small leaves. A 'Quatre Saisons'-type violet.

'**Baronne Alice de Rothschild**' (de Rothschild, France, 1894; 'Czar Bleu' seedling). Giant-flowered, mid-bluish-purple 86A-83A. Long stems. Early flowering. Thoroughly recommended. Also listed as 'Baron Rothschild' and 'Baroness Rothschild'; there is evidence that another single violet was being grown by at least one nursery, Bides of Farnham, Surrey, under the name 'Baron Louis de Rothschild' as both this and 'Baronne Alice de Rothschild' were separately listed in their 1931 catalogue. The name 'Baroness de Rothschild' has also been associated with a Parma violet. MRCF.

'**Beauty of Louth**' (Boothby, 1870).

'**Bechtel's Ideal**', see 'Ideal'.

'**Becky Groves**' (Groves, 2000). Pale to mid-pink, deeper centre.

'**Bernard's Pink**'. Warm pink 73D.

'Betty Hathaway' (Hathaway). Very deep plum-purple. Erect stems.

'Birmingham Belle' (Carman, New Zealand). No description available.

'Blackie' (Australia). Very dark purple approaching black.

'Bleu de Fontenay' (France, 1903; seedling developed from 'Quatre Saisons Semprez'). Deep violet blue with dark green foliage. Very hardy.

'Blue Bird', see 'Texas Tommy'.

'Blue Christmas' (Coombs, Winchester, Hampshire, 1969; 'Christmas' seedling). Pale blue flowers on short stems. Habit the same as 'Christmas'.

'Blue Emperor' (Australia). Large purple-blue flowers. Very strong perfume.

'Blue Gem' (Australia). Large purple flowers. Good perfume.

'Blue King'. Described as resembling 'Princesse de Galles' but brighter and more fragrant in the Fall 1926–Spring 1927 catalogue published by Carl Purdy of Ukiah, California.

'Blue Mrs R. Barton' (Coombs, 1966; 'Mrs R. Barton' seedling). Amethyst blue.

'Boston' (W. Sim, Cliftondale, Massachusetts, USA, 1908). Giant-flowered, lilac-blue, paler than 'Princesse de Galles'. Also allegedly freer-flowering, larger (4.5–5 cm/1 3/4–2 in across) but shorter (26.5–28 cm/10 1/2–11 in) and much thicker stems. Raised at reputedly the largest violet-growing establishment in the world at that time. Was W. Sim the William Sim of perpetual-flowering carnation fame? Although not widely listed in the UK, it did appear in Bunyards' 1924 list and probably others.

'Bournemouth Blue', 'Bournemouth Gem'. These names probably refer to the same cultivar; a selection from 'Governor Herrick' with large, slightly scented, purple-blue 86A-90A flowers, otherwise similar, and now rivalling it as the most widely grown commercial cultivar in England. Listed from 1947 onwards by Maurice Pritchard's Christchurch nurseries. See also pages 25 and 26.

'Braidwood' (Australia). No description available.

'Bright Mauve' (Australia). No description available.

'Brune de Bourg-la-Reine' (Millet, France, 1875; 'Le Lilas' x 'Czar'}. Large-flowered, purple with metallic sheen, so producing an ever-changing colour. Long, delicate green leaves. Strongly perfumed.

'Burgundy' (Australia). Rich burgundy flowers on a vigorous spreading plant.

'California' (Emery Smith, California, USA, 1892). According to George Saltford it created a sensation when the first flowers reached New York from California in blocks of ice. It was exported by Pitcher and Manda, Short Hills, New Jersey, and was first grown in France by Joseph Carbone. However, the American violet authority B. T. Galloway was convinced that it was the cultivar 'Mmc Emile Arène' (introduced in the South of France in 1891) but as it had so quickly acquired its new name, it would have caused confusion to change it. However, current practice now is that the earliest name should stand. Giant-flowered, dark violet-purple, giving the impression of a deep blue 93C, 3.75 cm (1¹/₂– 2 in) across on stems up to 35 cm (14 in) in length. Upper petals are somewhat pointed. Very hardy and sweetly scented. Free-flowering. An excellent cultivar. MRCF.

'Cardinale'. A very old cultivar still grown in France as a cut flower.

'Cendrillon' (France). A larger, but less free-flowering development from 'La Violette des Quatres Saisons'. Still grown in France and regarded as particularly hardy.

'Charles William Groves' (Groves, 1985; chance seedling found near 'Opera'). Good-sized magenta-pink 72C flowers with a purple reverse. Strong scent.

'Charm'. White. Has been grown in the USA.

'Chloe'. No description available.

'Christmas' (Margery Fish, c.1965). Very free-flowering white with the slightest tint of blue. Almost dwarf habit. A blue form was readily obtained as a seedling but was not listed by Margery Fish (see 'Blue Christmas').

'Clevedon Violet', see 'Victoria Regina'.

'Clive Groves' (Groves, 1980; chance seedling found near 'The Czar'). Vigorous plants with large reddish purple 83B flowers. Very fragrant.

'Coeur d'Alsace' (Millet, France, 1916; 'Rubra' x 'Le Lilas'). CM, FNHS. Unique rosy-salmon. For differing accounts of its origin see Chapter 7. Has been grown in the USA. Also listed as 'Cour d'Alsace'.

'Colombine' (Casbas, France, 1991; probably 'Czar' x form of 'Quatre Saisons'). Sky-blue flowers 97A.

'Comtesse Edmond du Tertre' (Molin, Lyon, France, c.1895). Large-flowered blue with long stems.

'Constance Apthorp' (Bunyard catalogue 1925–26). Listed in 1920s as a white cultivar, lightly flecked with pale blue. Vigorous and hardy.

'Copper Pennies' (Australia). No description available.

'Cordelia' (Dorothy Kimberley, Hereford, 1984; 'Coeur d'Alsace' seedling). White flowers with a palest pink blush and a mushroom-pink spur on long stems. Highly scented.

'Corfe Mullen Wonder' (Kettle, 1928). No description available.

'Corsican' (Margery Fish, c.1955). Coppery-lilac.

'Cottage Maid' (Carman, New Zealand). Pure white with slightest hint of mauve on reverse. Long stems. Compact growth.

'Cottle Stripe' (Bousfield, Launceston, Cornwall). Discovered in an orchard near Truro, Cornwall. Eye-catching plants with palest mauve flowers streaked and speckled with a darker mauve, pinkish-purple spur. Quite large. Faint perfume.

'Covent Garden' (Carman, New Zealand). Medium to large magenta flowers with darker eye.

'Crepuscle' (McLeod, NSW, Australia). Distinct large apricot flowers with mauve shading and a blue flush in the throat.

'**Crimaean**' (1870). Blue.

'**Crimson Bedder**' (1920). Listed by Kelways in 1921.

'**Culculata**' (Australia). Very vigorous with small rich red-violet flowers, very fragrant. The name is capable of causing confusion with *Viola cucullata (sororia).*

'**The Czar**' (Graham, 1863). FCC, RHS, 1865. Deep purple 86A-B with stems long enough for cutting. Free-flowering. Strong scent. An historic violet, the use of which in hybridization has resulted in many of the finest cultivars being produced. Also listed as 'Purple Czar'. MRCF.

'**Czar Bleu**' (Millet, 1878; seedling of 'The Czar'). Bluish-violet colour, still grown for cut-flower work in the south of France where it was renamed 'Reine Victoria' in honour of Queen Victoria who stayed there every year. Also listed as 'Victoria'.

'**Czar Rose**' (Casbas, France). A pink sport of 'Czar', was being grown in the 1920s.

'**Devonia**' (J. Heath, Kingskerswell, Devon, 1905). Large reddish-mauve 83A. Illustrated in 21 May 1910 issue of *The Garden*. Has been described as the finest of the red violets, being very sweetly scented and very vigorous.

'**Devoniensis**' (*c.*1860). Mid- to late-flowering, deep blue flowers formerly used for cutting. Its origins are unknown; the foliage was supposed to be similar to 'Wilson', but it was introduced before that cultivar came to France, let alone England. Nevertheless both 'Wilson' and 'Devoniensis' could have been forms of *Viola suavis* (see 'Russian'). 'Devoniensis' was described as the hardiest winter-blooming violet. It had produced a wealth of flowers throughout the winter of 1893–94 in a fully exposed position at Messrs Barr's Long Ditton Nursery near Surbiton in Surrey.[2]

'**Devon Red**'. Deep red.

'**Diana Groves**' (Groves, 1998; chance seedling). Large claret-red flowers.

'**Doctor Jameson**'. Listed by Kelways from 1903–29. See 'Kaiserin Augusta'.

'**Doe's Improved** (Barnham Nurseries, Sussex, from 1931). Probably a selected form of 'Princesse de Galles'.

'**Donau**' (Germany *c.*1925). Large dark blue 94B flowers with slight splash of white near base of lower petals and distinct bee lines. Compact habit.

'**Doreen**'. No description available.

'**Doris Bazeley**'. No description available. Exhibited at a meeting of the RHS on 9 February 1897 by H. Bazeley of Eastleigh, Hampshire.

'**Doris Sims**' (Australia). No description available.

'**Dorsett**' (P. H. Dorsett, Maryland, USA, 1910). The origins are referred to by B. T. Galloway in *Commercial Violet Culture*. Obtained as 'Princesse de Galles' but was wrongly named. Rich violet flowers of medium size. Very free-flowering. Rich dark green leaves.

'Dorset White' (1917).

'El Duende' (USA). Glowing crimson-purple. Neat, upright growth. Extremely fragrant.

'Elegantissima' (Carter, 1870). Blue.

'Elizabetha di Strassoldo'. Large-flowered blue.

'Elizabeth Bailes' (Margaret Howard, NSW, Australia). Soft lavender-pink flowers.

'Elizabeth Lee' (Burrows). Large violet flowers with white bases to petals. Long stems. Very vigorous.

'Elsie Coombs' (Windward Violet Nurseries; found among 'Rawson's White'). Discovered by the author of this book at the nurseries. Habit the same as 'Rawson's White' and only distinguishable by the unusual small Prussian blue zones at centre of the white flowers.

'Emilie Andre' (France, 1905). Similar to 'Kaiser Wilhelm II'.

'Empress' (Bernwode Plants, Buckinghamshire). Large flowers of a rich, deep plum colour. Very strong scent.

'Eton' (Turner, 1897). Clear blue. Rarely listed. Colour illustration in *Century Book of Gardening*.

'Excelsior' (1930). Listed by Wehrman, Germany 1961. No description available.

'Explorateur Dybowski' (Millet, France, 1893). Giant-flowered, deep blue with metallic sheen 86A-90A. Rather narrow petals. Long stems. Rather compact habit. Resistant to red spider mite attack. Compact growth. Believed to have been rediscovered in Queensland in 1996.

'Eynsford Giant' (Cannell, 1916). Very large-flowered blue.

'Fair Lady' (Carman, New Zealand). White flowers flushed and marked with soft lilac.

'Fair Oaks' (Whitlesey, California, USA, 1986). Small flowers on long stems. Delicate lilac pink 65C fading to near white. Lovely perfume.

'Fairy Wings', see 'Piglet'.

'Fashion'. Purple.

'Florence Lee' (Burrows). Medium-sized, royal-purple flowers. Long upper petals. Medium stems and small leaves. Late flowering and compact.

'Floribunda' (i) (Boothby, 1880; seedling of 'The Giant'). Bluish-purple. Very free flowering. (ii) (1910). Very similar to 'Princesse de Galles'.

'Frances Lee' (Burrows). Very large white flowers streaked with mauve. Medium-length stems. Mid-season.

'Frau Hedwig Bernock'. Listed by Kelways from 1909. No description available.

'Frau Hof Gartendirektor Jühlke' (Zeiner, Bornstedt, Potsdam, Germany, 1892; 'Victoria Regina' x 'Russian Superb'). Large-flowered light blue. Exceptionally free-flowering. Powerful fragrance. Has been recommended for cutting. Very bright green foliage. Suitable for training as a tree violet. Listed by Clibrans from 1894.

'Frederica'. No description available.

'French Grey' (1965). This, or another cultivar with the same name, was listed in the 1950s and 1960s by Margery Fish. Pale lavender 92C. It should be noted that the hardy double cultivar 'Comte de Chambord' has been grown under this name.

'Frey's Fragrant' (Frey, USA, 1925; 'Governor Herrick' seedling). Scentless or nearly so despite its name, it was grown extensively for cutting in the USA and is still being grown at Rhinebeck.[3]

'Germania' (c.1890). No description available.

'The Giant' (1860). Bluish-purple. Grown quite widely in Canada and Britain as well as the USA where it was regarded as having somewhat larger flowers than 'The Czar', produced more freely. The blooms were up to 2.5 cm (1 in) in diameter. It is believed that this cultivar may have survived at the Año-Nuevo Flower Farm in California since 1901.

'Giant Elk', see 'Royal Elk' (Pawla, USA). Large-flowered blue with very long stems. Grown in the USA in recent years. The cultivar listed as 'Royal Elk' is probably identical.

'Giantess' (Boothby, 1873). White.

'Giuletto Fanin' (Fanin, Italy). Very vigorous with large blue flowers.

'Glabella', see 'Sulfurea'.

'Gloire de Bourg-la-Reine' (Millet, France, 1879; seedling of 'The Czar'). Very large-flowered, bluish-purple. Long stems. The first Millet seedling to have rounded petals. Unlike most large-flowered violets, seed was quite freely produced. Large dark green foliage with marked denticulation. Subtle, sweet perfume.

'Gloire de France' (France, 1905). Large-flowered, reddish-mauve. Listed by Bunyards from 1908.

'Gloire d'Hyères' (France, 1898). Deep blue.

'Goodwin's Blue' (Australia).

'Gothic'. No description available.

'Governor Herrick' (USA, 1910). Deep bluish-purple 86A. Unscented, although it was described as very sweetly scented by Blackmore and Langdon in 1916 soon after its introduction to Britain. The cultivar cannot have been named before 1904, as Governor Herrick of Ohio was elected in that year. It is very resistant to red spider mite attack and the flowers last longer when cut than the scented singles.

'Graf Molkte' (Germany, c.1897). Dark blue with tendency to fade. Reputedly disease-resistant and resistant to red spider mite.

'Grandiflora' (1910). Giant-flowered blue. Rounded petals.

'Granny Marsh' (Australia). Small pale blue. Bright green foliage.

'Greyfriar's Bobby' (Carman, New Zealand). Very distinct colour between smoky-grey and mauve.

'Grey Lady' (Australia). Pale lilac-grey flowers. Good perfume.

'Hamburger' (Germany, 1890). Blue. This cultivar produced a number of different forms.

'Hedwig Bernock' (Germany, c.1925). Very hardy dark blue, flowering freely from autumn onwards.

'Helen Hyatt' (Australia). No description available.

'Helvetia' (Millet, France, 1914). Large-flowered lilac.

'Highland Lassie' (Carman, New Zealand). Deep purple, almost black in centre. Deep green foliage.

'House's White'. According to Mrs Grace L. Zambra this was a small-flowered cultivar without a great deal of scent and difficult to grow. However, in later years it was referred to in the list issued by her Windward Violet Nurseries as a synonym of 'Rawson's White' though the two do not appear similar, the latter being a strong grower as could be confirmed by the plants still growing at Windward in the 1980s.

'Ideal' (Bechtel, Germany, 1910). Blue violet formerly used for forcing in time for St Valentine's Day (*Gartnerborse and Gartenwelt*, 1986).

'Immaculata' (Australia). No description available.

'Imperatrice Augusta', see 'Kaiserin Augusta'.

'Imperial White' (1875).

'Irene', see 'Köningen Charlotte'.

'Irish Elegance', see 'Sulfurea'.

'Ishtar' (Bousefield, Launceston, Cornwall). Very bright lavender 87-88B flowers on long stems.

'Italia' (Italy, 1896; 'Princess Beatrice' seedling). Deep blue. It attracted favourable comment when exhibited by Isaac House and Son at Brighton in December 1897.

'Jack Sampson' (Australia).

'Jean Arnot' (Windward Violet Nurseries, 1983). (Australia). Two of the original divisions, propagated by the author of this book, of the cultivar later known as 'Princess Diana' were different in colour though this had not been noticed during the previous flowering season. A very large-flowered old rose-pink 58D-62A on long stems suitable for picking. Perhaps unique.

'Jennifer's Pink' (Bousfield, Launceston, Cornwall). A pale, cool pink.

'Jen's Purple' (The Fragrant Garden, NSW, Australia). No description available.

'John Raddenbury' (Australia, 1895). Mid-blue 94C with the possibility of a rosy flush on alkaline soils. Strong scent. It has been grown as a market cut flower with successful results; however, only a small number of flowers are produced in the autumn. Also listed as 'John Raddenburg' probably because the handwritten 'y' of J. J. Kettle, who did much to popularize this cultivar, could easily be mistaken for a 'g'. Probably named after John Raddenberry (or Raddenbury), the second curator of the Geelong

Botanical Gardens in Victoria.[4]

'Josephine' (Carman, New Zealand). Carmine-cerise 81C.

'Juwell' (Teicher, Germany, 1932). Dark blue flowers.

'Kaiserin Augusta' (Rathke and Sohn, Praust, Germany, c.1885; Reputedly 'Semperflorens' x *Viola rossica*). Dark blue 92A. Early flowering.

'Kaiserin Augusta Viktoria' (H. Wrede, Luneburg, Germany, c.1895). Compact habit. Dark crimson flowers. Also listed as 'Doctor Jameson' and 'Reine Augustine'.

'Kaiserin Friedrich' (Alfred Hoede, Erfurt, Germany, 1911). Purplish-blue.

'Kaiserin von Osterreich'. Crimson-red flowers.

'Kaiser Wilhelm II' (Germany, 1895). AM, RHS, 1913. Giant-flowered, deep bluish-purple flowers up to 4.5 cm (1¾ in) across. Probably the most strongly scented single violet, it has been grown on a very large scale in Devon and elsewhere for cutting. Plants of a selected stock of this cultivar were given the name 'King of the Belgians' (sometimes 'King Albert') during World War I by F. E. Dillistone who claimed that they had an increased resistance to red spider mite attack and that he had obtained the permission of King Albert of the Belgians to so name it. Both these claims may well be true, but it is highly dubious whether this change of name is valid. I always sold runners of this cultivar as 'Kaiser Wilhelm II' as intended by the raiser, this being in line with current horticultural practice. MRCF.

'Katja'. Bright. warm pink, shaded red 60D with pencilled lines in centre.

'Kerry Girl'. (Carman, New Zealand). Lavender-pink 65C with distinctive lines on lower petals. Very large and free-flowering.

'King Albert', see 'Kaiser Wilhelm II'.

'King of the Belgians', see 'Kaiser Wilhelm II'.

'Knockmullen' (1910). Bluish-purple. Described as an earlier and freer-flowering 'Wellsiana'.

'Köningin Charlotte' (Germany, 1900). Very fragrant blue 90B-88C. Very early flowering, from August onwards, and very free. A cultivar of the 'Quatre Saisons' type with flowers looking up into the sky. Regarded at The Violet Nurseries, Henfield, and by Barrs as an improvement on 'California', but this view (which could indicate that wrongly named stocks were being commented on as 'California' or 'Madame Emile Arene') was not widely shared. Also listed as 'Irene'.

'Kronprinzessin von Deutschland' (Germany c.1885). Very large, early, crimson-violet flowers on long stems. Not very hardy.

'Lady Clifford' (1903; raised at Ugbrook Park, Chudleigh, Devon – the home of the Clifford family). Similar to 'Princesse de Galles' except that the giant flowers were shaded with purple and had a more clearly defined white eye, the flowers were earlier, the habit more compact and the stems shorter (25 cm/10 in).

'**Lady Jayne**' (Windward Violet Nurseries, 1983). Deep rich purple with reddish sheen 86B. Long stems. Very free-flowering and a strong grower.

'**Lady Rose**' (Australia; 'Rosina' sport). Pure clear rose-pink. Strong perfume.

'**La France**' (Millet, France, 1891; 'Gloire de Bourg-la-Reine' seedling). There are references to the parentage being 'Gloire de Bourg-la-Reine' x 'Princesse de Galles' or even the reverse cross, and the date of raising has been stated as being 1891. AM, RHS, 1900. Giant flowers of deep bluish-purple with a metallic sheen 86A. Fairly long stems. Has been grown in the USA. Possibly rediscovered in France.

'**La Grande Luxonne**', see 'Madame Emile Arène'.

'**La Grosse Bleue**' (France, 1895). This was, as its name revealed, a large-flowered blue violet.

'**Lamb's White**' (Lamb's Nursery, Spokane, Washington, USA, 1985). Pure white flowers produced freely over a long season.

'**Lancashire Lad**' (Carman, New Zealand). Large, dark purple-blue fading with age. Early.

'**L'Arne**', see 'Lianne'.

'**Laurel Knoll**' (Australia). Pink flowers.

'**Lavender Lady**'. Pale lavender 82C flowers with long upper petals. Very vigorous and very fragrant.

'**Lavender Mist**' (The Fragrant Garden, NSW, Australia).

'**Lee's Blue**' (Burrows). Soft violet blue 86D with long, narrow petals.

'**Lee's Ivory**' (Burrows). A superb violet. The largest of the 'white' single violets. Suitable for cut-flower work.

'**Lee's Peachy Pink**' (Burrows).

'**Lee's Pink**' (Burrows). Ivory shaded old rose 62C.

'**Le Lilas**' (Millet, France, 1876). Heliotrope lilac, an unusual colour. Early and free-flowering. Parent of several pink, lilac and purple cultivars.

'**Lianne**' (France 1903). Deep bluish-purple with carmine tints 83A-80A. Flowers of medium size only but produced from September until April. Strongly scented. Has been used for cut-flower work in northern France. Mrs Grace L. Zambra considered this cultivar was at its best in thin woodland so possibly use as ground cover in shrubberies if not too dense.

'**Lilac Glow**' (Australia).

'**L'Inépuisable**' (France, 1899; 'The Czar' x 'Quatre Saisons Semprez'). Purplish-blue. Semi-perpetual flowering: August until May. Mrs Grace L. Zambra wrote that it soon exhausted their patience at the Windward Violet Nurseries (despite its name). However, cultivars of the 'Quatre Saisons' type are no longer common and it may be useful for hybridizing. It was noted that it tended to fade later in the season.

'**Lise Lazare**' (Giulio Fanin, Udine, Italy). Discovered in an old garden. Large blue flowers.

'**Little Papoose**' (USA). Greyish-rose.

'**Lobelia**' (Kettle, 1928). No description available.

'**London**' (1869). Blue. One of the first cultivars of the Russian violet to be grown for the London flower markets, hence its name. Small blue flowers on dwarf plants. Many runners. Free-flowering in the spring.

'**Lubecker**' (Germany, c.1895).

'**Lutea**', see 'Sulfurea'.

'**Luxonne**' (Millet, France, c.1888; 'Wilson' x 'The Czar'). Large-flowered bluish-purple 90A. MRCF. 'Luxonne Bonnifoy' and 'Luxonne Parimon' were supposedly improved forms named after their originators, both being introduced in 1895.

'**Lydia Groves**' (Groves, 1989; 'Coeur d'Alsace' sport). Sugar pink 69A sometimes streaked with rose. Free-flowering. Strong scent.

'**Lydia's Legacy**' (Groves, 1999; 'Lydia Groves' sport). Bright cerise sometimes splashed with purple.

'**Mme** (or **Mlle**) **Armandine Pagès**' (France, 1900). Very pale rose-pink 62C with carmine centre. Strong perfume. Semi-perpetual flowering.

'**Mme Emile Arène**' (France, 1895; 'Luxonne' seedling). Very large deep-blue flowers. Highly regarded by some growers in the south of France. B. T. Galloway believed this cultivar was 'renamed' 'California'. See also 'California'.

'**Mme Fichet-Nardy**' (France, 1906). Deep blue. Very free-flowering.

'**Mme Laredo**' (Millet, 'Amiral Avellan' seedling). No description available.

'**Mme Noélie**' (France, 1906). Large-flowered blue with carmine tints. Distinctive long stems above flowers. One of the most free-flowering cultivars I grew in Winchester. Also listed as 'Aubéreinne', 'Trinité' and 'Noélie'.

'**Mme Rose Borne**' (France, 1906; 'Mme Fichet-Nardy' seedling). Very deep-violet flowers.

'**Mme Schwartz**' (1906). Large-flowered blue. May still be grown in France. Has been recommended for colder districts. At one time described by Kelways of Langport, Somerset, as the best single violet. Listed by Frikart 1950.

'**Mlle Alamagny**' (France, 1906; 'Mme Fichet-Nardy' seedling). Reddish-purple.

'**Mlle Antoinette Fichet-Nardy**' (France, 1906; 'Mme Fichet-Nardy' seedling). Reddish-purple.

'**Mlle Bonnefoy**' (Millet, France, c.1930; 'Le Lilas' seedling).

'**Mlle Garrido**' (Millet, France, 1914). Large-flowered lilac rose.

'**Mlle Louise Tricheux**' (Millet, France; 'White Czar' seedling).

'**Mlle Susanne Lemarquis**' (Millet, France, c.1930).

'**Margaret Hayley**' (c.1930). Deep pink.

'Marguerite di Savoie' (i) (1895). Large-flowered, bluish-mauve. (ii) (1925). White. See also Parma violet 'Principessa di Savoie'.

'Marietta' (Millet, France, 1914). Mid-blue.

'Maroon' (Windward Violet Nurseries, c.1981). See 'Lady Jayne'. Renamed at the West Winds Nursery.

'Marquis de Brazais' (France). Medium-sized violet flowers. Possibly still grown in France.

'Meizner Madel' (Germany, 1930). Deep blue.

'Mignonette' (Millet, France, 1876; 'The Czar' x 'Wilson'). FCC, FNHS. Large-flowered blue 90D. One of the first of Armand Millet's seedlings, later renamed 'Souvenir de Millet père'. It should be noted that a very free-flowering bluish white cultivar was listed by an English nursery under the latter name in the early 1900s, when other nurseries were still offering the original blue cultivar.

'Millet père', see 'Mignonette'.

'Miss America' (Pawla, USA). Very large, soft lavender. Long stems. Very fragrant. Described as a favourite show cultivar. Related to 'California' and 'Princesse de Galles'.

'Miss Cannell' (Cannell, c.1890s). No description available.

'Miss Ethel Lewis'. No description available. Exhibited by A. A. C. Lewis, Bedgebury Park, Goudhurst, Kent, at a meeting of the RHS on 11 April 1905.

'Miss Naylor'. No description. Exhibited by Mr Kent, Dean House Gardens, Alresford, Hampshire, at a meeting of the RHS on 14 February 1905.

'Mistress Mallory' (Carman, New Zealand). Large rose-pink, paler at edges of petals. Later flowering.

'Monsieur Villard' (1879). No description available. Found in Madame Vachin's garden at Ecully, Rhone.

'Montgomery's White' (1910). White flowers with a very sweet perfume. Although not widely grown in England, this cultivar was probably raised at Fivemiletown, Ireland, and may have been more popular there.

'Mother of Pearl' (Robert Peace, Victoria, Australia). Pale blue flowers.

'Mother's Day' (Mary Mottram, North Molton, Devon). Distinct white cultivar with small warm mauve markings at base of petals.

'Moyser' (Freund, Silesia, Germany, c.1895). Dark blue flowers on long stems. Large dark green leaves. Flowered abundantly in November and December.

'Mr Gladstone' (1905). Large-flowered blue.

'Mrs F. B. Dwight' (1939). Giant-flowered deep violet-blue. Claimed to have larger flowers on stems nearly as long (25–38 cm/10–15 in) and of better quality and in greater numbers than 'Princesse de Galles'. Mrs Grace L. Zambra wrote in the issue of *Amateur Gardening* dated 2 January 1951 that it came from Cornwall and was definitely better than either 'Princesse de Galles' or any cultivars produced by Armand Millet. Still listed in the

1. Alice Witter
2. Queensland Violet
3. Pamela Zambra
4. Governor Herrick
5. Cuccullata
6. Bournemouth Gem

early 1960s, and according to Roy Genders was being grown in the Falmouth area of Cornwall more recently.[5] MRCF.

'Mrs Pinchurst' (*c*.1930). Large-flowered blue of the 'Governor Herrick' type[6]. Still grown in France. Similar colour to 'Pamela Zambra' but larger and without runners.

'Mrs R. Barton' (Windward Violet Nurseries, *c*.1930; 'Princesse de Galles' seedling). White ground with violet markings of variable intensity. 'Alassio', 'Constance Apthorp' and 'Marguerite di Savoie' (ii), could be synonymous. Very free-flowering, stems long enough for cutting although somewhat weak. Mr Barton was the foreman of the Windward Violet Nurseries; Mrs Barton was the cook working for the Zambras; and at one time it seemed as if most of the Barton family worked in the nurseries. This cultivar readily produces seed, many of which are true, and the remainder produce the amethyst-violet form sold by the author as 'Blue Mrs Barton'.

'Mrs Reid's French Violet' (Bousfield, Launceston, Cornwall). Discovered by Moyra Reid in France. Purplish-claret 75A. Reputed to be a form of 'Rubra'.

'Muhlberg' (Germany, *c*.1895). No description available.

'Nana Compacta' (France, 1903). Deep blue. Similar habit to 'Lianne'.

'New Red Wine' (Pawla, USA). Medium-sized flowers on quite long stems above light green foliage.

'Noélie', see 'Madame Noélie'.

'Noni' (Kimberley, Hereford).

'Norah Church' (Windward Violet Nurseries. *c*.1930). Very early-flowering, silvery-amethyst 77B, seedling collected from the wild. Nice erect stems above distinct foliage.

'Northcourt' (1911). Probably raised at Torquay, Devon. Rose-pink with pale mauve centre.

'Odoratissima' (Lee, 1877). Pale slate blue. Almost circular flowers with rounded petals. Strong perfume.

'Opal Prince' (McLeod, NSW, Australia). Opalescent clear reddish-pink flowers. Very fragrant.

'Opéra' (*c*.1930). Lilac-mauve with pale blue shading and rose centre 77B-80A.

'Orchid Pink' (Margery Fish, *c*.1960). Palest mauve 74D, deepening towards the centre. An unusual and beautiful violet.

'Otto Glagau' (Germany, *c*.1905). Dark blue flowers above elegant and luxuriant foliage. Blooms January onwards.

'Pale Blush' (McLeod, NSW, Australia).

'Pallida', see 'Sulfurea'; 'Pallida plena', see 'Neapolitan' (Parma violet list). There is also a distinct species of viola with this name.

'Palmer's Violet' (1956). No description. This cultivar was being assessed as a cultivar for market work at the Experimental Horticultural Station, Rosewarne, Camborne, Cornwall.

'Palustris'. White. Has been grown in the USA in recent years. There is also a distinct species, *Viola palustris*.

'Pamela Zambra' (Windward Violet Nurseries, *c*.1930; 'Explorateur Dybowski' seedling). Large flowers of violet-blue, shading to purple 96A-90A. Any trace of scent vanishes within an hour or so of picking. Late flowering. Lasts well in water and almost immune from red spider mite attack. (See also page 26.)

'Pat Toolan's Red' (Australia).

'Perle Rose' (France, 1902; 'Rubra' seedling). Medium-sized flowers of an eye-catching deep coral-rose 64D. Compact habit. Probably the latest of the scented singles to flower, thereby usefully extending the season.

'Philadelphia' (USA, 1895). Blue. Sweetly scented.

'Phyll Dove' (Australia; 'Sulfurea' sport). Orange-coloured flowers.

'Pierre Benite' (France, 1895). No description available. Has been grown in England.

'Piglet' (McLeod, NSW, Australia). Subtle lilac-grey flowers freely produced.

'Pineapple Gleam'. No description available.

'Pink Perle', see 'Perle Rose'.

'President Cleveland' (1903). Deep blue. This cultivar, presumably of American origin, was listed in the Froebel catalogue.

'Pretoria Violet', see 'Wilson'.

'Primavera' (Italy, 1890). Very large-flowered deep blue. Attracted attention when exhibited at the Brighton Show by Isaac House and Son in December 1897.

'Prince Consort' (Lee, 1876). Deep purple.

'Prince of Wales', see 'Princesse de Galles'.

'Princess Alexandra' (1913). Deep reddish-purple. Sometimes claimed as being an improvement on 'Amiral Avellan', but the two seem quite distinct, this cultivar having a shorter flowering season and being somewhat less hardy, but making up for this with an unfading colour and stouter stems. Sometimes listed as 'Amiral de Breton'. See also 'Alexandra'.

'Princess Beatrice'. Giant-flowered, very bright blue, 3.75 cm (1 1/2 in) across on fairly long 23-cm (9-in) stems. Exhibited at an RHS meeting in 1898 and received the Award of Merit. The exhibitor, Mr Nobbs, Queen Victoria's gardener at Osborne House on the Isle of Wight, claimed that he had discovered this violet in an uncared-for part of the grounds there and that Queen Victoria had named it after her youngest daughter. However, Armand Millet stated its raiser to be M. Molin of Lyon, France.[7] Although conceivably it could have been imported from England, the fact that Mr Bunyard stated that it had been found as a chance seedling in a bed of 'The

Czar' growing in the south of France in 1888,[8] seems to support the claim that the violet is of French origin unless, of course, two violets were involved.

'**Princess Diana**' (Windward Violet Nurseries, 1982; possibly a seedling of 'Rosea Delicatissima' or 'Madame Armandine Pagès'). The original plant was found and propagated at the nurseries by the author of this book; I divided the plant of this giant-flowered pale pink 65B violet, which has no trace of mauve or blue tints, into seven pieces. Two of the divisions appeared to have changed colour when next in flower, resulting in an urgent telephone call from the nurseries to my home in Honiton. The original coloured form was subsequently listed as 'Princess Diana' and the deeper sport as 'Jean Arnot'. Another nursery, after selling the plants as 'Princess Diana' for one year, then changed the name to 'Jean Arnot', due to concerns over the legality of this cultivar's name, which meant that two quite distinct, though closely related, violets were being offered for sale under the same name in different nursery lists; the matter had clearly not been thought through. Jean Arnot's accounts of the origins of these two cultivars have been published in the Devon NCCPG book *The Magic Tree* and in *Sweet Times* (see Bibliography) and exactly tally with my own recollections.

'**Princesse de Galles**' (Millet, France, 1889; 'Gloire de Bourg-la-Reine' seedling according to Millet. AM, RHS 1895). Giant-flowered lilac-blue 88C-B. Probably internationally the most extensively grown scented cultivar, definitely so in the UK. MRCF.

'**Princess of Prussia**' (Lee, 1881). Purple.

'**Princess of Wales**', see 'Princesse de Galles'.

'**Princess Victoria**' (1924). Pale purple.

'**Principessa di Summunte**' (Bredemeier, Italy, 1895). FCC, FNHS 1899. White ground flaked with pale blue. This cultivar may have been a single-flowered Parma (see also page 72, 73 and 76). Also listed as 'Princesse de Sumante', sometimes spelt Sumonte, Soumonte, Sumente.

'**Purple Czar**', see '(The) Czar'.

'**Quaker Lady**' (Pawla, USA). Small bluish-lilac flowers with white centre. Good scent. Imported from England during the pioneer days.

'**Quatre Saisons**' (Chevillion, France, 1830). Pale, rather dull, lilac-blue. Semi-perpetual flowering and whatever the month, the flowers are very sweetly scented; as a writer in the *Journal of Horticulture and Home Farmer* put it: 'This variety is exceptional not only in the perpetual flowering habit but in its profuse flowering; it should surely be called multiflora as its flowers are positively thrown up by the thousand starting soon after midsummer and continuing with little intermission till May.' J. C. House told a meeting of the Royal Horticultural Society in 1917 how he had purchased rooted cuttings at one shilling (5p) each in the spring and by July they were good clumps smothered with blossom for which a florist offered him five shillings (25p) each. Most growers have considered this cultivar to be synonymous to 'Semperflorens'. However, Mrs Grace L. Zambra wrote that although they were supposed to be identical, they were actually distinct, as 'Semperflorens' was far better. There were several other forms varying in colour and freedom and duration of flowering, one of the most distinct being the one with white flowers. The plants of 'Semperflorens' I used to sell originated from stock I obtained from Thornton Heath, Surrey, where it had been grown for many years. Pale lilac-blue 94B flowers in Winchester would first be produced in August and continue to the spring, and the cultivar set seed which came true to type.

'Queen Alexandra' (1906). Large-flowered very rich ultramarine. One of the earliest to start flowering. Lovely perfume.

'Queen Charlotte', see 'Köningin Charlotte'.

'Rawson's White' (Rawson, 1888). Free-flowering white, the early flowers being tinged with pink. Deep green foliage. Supposed to be an improved form of *Viola odorata alba*. The raiser, one of the leading amateur violet growers, was Vicar of Bromley, Kent, and later Felsbarrow, Windermere. This cultivar has been grown in the USA. 'House's White' is considered to be a synonym in the last lists issued by the Windward Violet Nurseries in the 1960s.

'Red Charm' (1955). Reddish-salmon 60D.

'Red Lion' Magenta 77B-70B flowers fading to lightish-pink as the season advances. Delicate perfume. Plants have reached the UK from both Australia and the USA.

'Red Queen' (1958). Deep crimson-purple 72A. It has been described as a red form of 'Coeur d'Alsace'.

'Red Russian', see 'Russian'.

'Reid's Crimson Carpet' (John Whitlesey, California, USA, 1998). Compact plant with tidy deep green foliage. Brilliant crimson 78B flowers with a lovely scent.

'Reine Augustine', see 'Kaiserin Augusta'.

'Reine Victoria', see 'Czar Bleu'.

'Reise von Botnang' (1930). No description available.

'Riviera Violet'. A pale blue now believed to be distinct from 'St Helena'.

'Rochelle' (Pawla, USA). Free-flowering over a long period. Very fragrant small rose-pink.

'Rohrbach's Everblooming'. Purple flowers.

'Rosanna' Distinct dusky-warm pink 67B.

'Rosea Delicatissima' (Millet, France, 1914). Pale rose-pink.

'Rose Madder' (Bernwode Plants, Buckinghamshire). Large-flowered soft rose-pink.

'Rose Perle', see 'Perle Rose'.

'Rosie' (Carman, New Zealand). Rose fading to mother-of-pearl at edges. Deep green foliage. Compact plants.

'Rosine' (Durez, 1920). Selected form of the pink 63B sweet violet, *Viola odorata rosea*. It has been used as a market cut flower. Very sweet perfume. Very popular in the 1920s and 1930s. It is still grown in Britain and the USA. AM, RHS, 1924. Also listed as 'Rosina'.

'Royal Ascot' (Carman, New Zealand). Large light smoky-amethyst. Free-flowering. Very long flowering season.

'Royal Elk' (Pawla, USA, *c*.1947). Deep purplish-blue flowers up to 5 cm (2 in) across on 23–30-cm (9–12-in) stems and with a lovely perfume. Recently rediscovered by John Whittlesey in a San Francisco garden.

'Royal Robe' (Pawla, USA, *c*.1947). Large, deep purplish-blue 87A. Obtained by the Windward Violet Nurseries from another Cornish nursery and now quite easily available in the UK. Large scented flowers similar to 'Royal Elk'. Possibilities for cut-flower work. (*Viola* 'Purple Robe' (*V. gracilis* x *V. cornuta* 'Papillio', mentioned in *Gardeners Chronicle* 28 October 1911).

'Rubra' (L. Paillet, Châtenay-les-Sceaux, France, 1881). Late-flowering rosy-red 78A. Listed by Maurice Pritchard's Christchurch, Hampshire nurseries and then by my Winchester nurseries. Now quite widely listed in the UK.

'Russian'. (i) Species from Russia. Probably no longer grown. Improved form **'Russian Superb'** (1873) with larger flowers was still listed in early 1960s. (ii) Paler Russian form, *Viola suavis* or *V. tauria*. Probably no longer in cultivation. (iii) 'White Russian' (1869). White. Grown widely before the introduction of 'White Czar'. Probably no longer in cultivation. (iv) 'Red Russian' (1905). Reddish-copper. Still in cultivation in 1930s. (v) 'Pritchard's Russian'. Large purple with greyish sheen listed by Maurice Pritchard and Son from 1925 onwards, but may be much older. Then, as with 'Rubra', it was obtainable from my Winchester nurseries and it is now quite widely listed.

'St Anne's' (1900). Rosy-red. Attracted attention when exhibited by Isaac House and Son at the Kent Chrysanthemum Show in Margate, November 1902. It has been claimed that 'Red Queen' might be a reintroduction of this violet. Also listed as 'St Anne's Pink' and 'St Anne's Red'. It is difficult to reconcile Graham Stuart Thomas's description: 'That charmer in soft rosy hue'[9] with that in the catalogue of Ballards of Colwall, Worcestershire: 'Deep ruby red form of the wild white violet', so possibly these were distinct cultivars.

'St Augustine' (USA, 1892). Blue, being described as very similar to 'Schönbrunn'. Found by Mrs J. L. Gardner near St Augustine, Florida.

'St Helena' (1897). Pale lavender-blue 97A-B. This cultivar has been highly praised. A. T. Johnson described it thus: 'Among the sweet violets there is none so indescribably lovely, nor quite so well-bred, as the "St Helena" violet whose origin is as mysterious as its name. This exquisite thing creeps about much as do the rest of its household but with more constraint, and among its pale green leaves appear throughout the spring a succession of very fragrant violets in the delicatest of blues. The colour and fragrance have been distilled to a point of refinement seldom attained by mortals.'[10] And again: 'The winsome "St Helena" whose flowers "cool as water, soft as sleep", in the tenderness of their bog violet blue are ineffably sweet.'[11] Gertrude Jekyll has written of its 'pale blue colour never seen in wild or other garden kinds', and James C. House, whose firm did much to popularize it, wrote that it produced quantities of sky-blue flowers in the sharpest weather. With regard to its origin 'G.J.' (Gertrude Jekyll?) wrote in the 20 March 1920 issue of *The Garden* that it was in full bloom in mid-February and was given her nearly 50 years before by an old lady living on the outskirts of a country village. 'G.J.' speculated that it might have come from the island of St Helena, and mentioned that its perfume was a little stronger than the typical *Viola odorata* and that it was earlier flowering. Edward A. Bunyard has written that it was also known as the Riviera violet which could have been another clue to supposed Napoleonic origins but these violets are now considered to be distinct. Although several growers have referred to it having a completely novel colour, unfortunately none seem to have grown other pale blue cultivars, and possibly had they done so, the colour would not have seemed so original. 'Mignonette' has rarely been grown in Britain but of course 'John Raddenbury' has; the Windward Violet Nurseries catalogue was one of the very few that listed both 'John Raddenbury' and 'St Helena', so enabling a comparison to be made: the former, described as china blue, had larger flowers and came into flower later than 'St Helena' which was described as very pale blue and flowering over a long season.

'**Sans Pareille**' (Millet, France, 1880). Large-flowered blue with rounded petals. Described as being of 'The Czar' type. FCC, FCHS 1880.

'**Sans Prix**' (Millet, France, 1880). No description available.

'**Schönbrunn**' (1887). Blue.

'**Schone von Botnang**' (Germany, *c*.1925). Dark blue flowers, freely produced.

'**Schubert**' (Present in the New Zealand National Collection.)

'**Schwabenmatchen**' (Germany, *c*.1925). No description available.

'**Schwabenstolz**' (Germany, *c*.1925). No description available.

'**Semperflorens**', '**Semperflorens Alba**', see 'Quatre Saisons'.

'**Semprez**' (Semprez, Verrières, France, 1898). Blue. A 'Quatre Saisons' cultivar at one time grown in some quantity for the Paris market.

'**Shot Silk**' (Australia). No description available.

'**Sisters**' (Groves, 1998; 'Lydia Groves' x 'Rawson's White'). White flowers with a blush of pink 75D-76D.

Viola odorata (drawing by Yvonne Matthews).

'**Sky Blue**' (Lamb Nurseries, Spokane, Washington, USA, 1959). Free-flowering, large, sky-blue.

'**Smith's Seedling**' (1900). No description available.

'**Souvenir de Jules Josse**' (Etablissement Hubert, Midi, France, 1902). Deep reddish-mauve 77A-B, very large flowers, 3.75cm (1½ in) across. Still listed in the early 1960s and now available again. Also listed as 'Souvenir de Jean Josse', 'Sou de San Jose' and 'Aubéreinne'.

'**Souvenir de Ma Fille**' (Millet, France, 1912; 'Cyclope' x 'La France'). CM, FNHS, 1914. Giant-flowered, deep blue, grown on a large scale for cutting in the years immediately following its introduction.

'**Souvenir de Millet père**', see 'Mignonette'.

'**Steel Blue**' (Kettle, 1928). No description available.

'**Suffolk Lady**' (Carman, New Zealand). No description available.

'**Sulfurea**' (France, 1896). The so-called yellow sweet violet, which is in fact neither yellow nor sweet. The creamy primrose flowers with deep apricot 8C centres are very attractive and, apart from lack of perfume, resemble the sweet violets. Dark green foliage. It is almost certainly a distinct species and appears in the list of species in Chapter 6. There is a possibility that more than one plant may have been cultivated under this name as W. E. Th Ingwersen, VMH, writing in 1951, mentioned having been given a buff-coloured form with delightfully sweet flowers. See also 'Crepuscule' and 'Phyll Dove'.

'**Sweet Petite Blue**' (Pawla, USA). Small deep-blue flowers on compact plants.

'**Tanith**' (Bousfield). Large white flowers with a slight blush on early flowers and a buff spur.

'**Tauria**', see 'Russian'.

'**Tenerife Violet**', see 'Wilson'.

'**Texas Tommy**' Light blue. Has been grown in the USA. Also listed as 'Blue Bird'.

'**Theophilus Lee**' (Burrows). Large plum-coloured flowers with white eye on long stems. Vigorous habit.

'**Thomas**' (Mary Mottram, North Molton, Devon). No description available.

'**Tina Whitaker**' (Baldwin Pinney, Marehurst, Kent, 1922). Found in a garden at Palermo, Sicily. Giant-flowered amethyst 77B flowers up to 5.75cm (2 ¼ in) across which have been stated as lasting for up to three weeks in water. The shape of the flowers was elongated and unrefined ñ 'somewhat the appearance of a poor viola' was part of the description in 15 March 1922 issue of *The Garden*, and the petals were thin and pointed. However, Mrs Grace L. Zambra referred to it as 'amazingly lovely' and thought it to be the most beautiful cultivar. It has been grown commercially in Cornwall but its widespread cultivation has been prevented by difficulties with its propagation. It is still listed and although it grows best under glass, despite its faults it has been recommended by the Ministry of Agriculture as an outdoor commercial cut-flower cultivar.

'Trinité', see 'Madame Noélie'.

'Titania' Pale pink flowers with a slight flush of darker pink 69A &65C as on reverse of petals. Strong perfume but the flower stems are rather weak.

'Triumph' (1945). Large-flowered lilac-blue with a compact habit similar to that of 'Princess Beatrice'. Long stems suitable for cutting. Rich perfume. It has been grown in Switzerland. Listed by Blooms Nurseries in 1961.

'Truscott's Pink' Large clear pink 75A.

'Victoria' (1905) Blue. Listed by Forbes of Hawick, Scotland. This cultivar may have been 'Czar Bleu' ('Reine Victoria'). Still grown in France as 'Chambers' Victoria', see Chapter 3.

'Victoria Regina' (Lee, 1873; 'The Czar' x 'Devoniensis'). Deep-violet 79B flowers on compact plants.

'Victory' (F. J. Graham, Cranford, Middlesex, 1870). Purple. Described as larger, better-shaped and more fragrant than the same raiser's 'The Czar'. It was also supposed to be suitable for training as a tree violet.

'Victory Violet' (Pawla, USA). Giant, rich velvety violet flowers up to 6 cm (2½ in) across on stems up to 30 cm (12 in) long. Pleasing sweet fragrance.

'Vilmorinia', see 'Sulfurea'.

'Violet Lady' (McLeod, NSW, Australia). Dark violet flowers. Very fragrant and vigorous.

'Wellsiana' (Mr Wells, Fern Hill, Windsor). FCC, RHS, 1884, and also an important award at the Manchester Show in the same year. Large flowers up to 2.5 cm (1 in) across, bluish-purple with carmine tints. Edward A. Bunyard wrote that its bronzy-blue colour was rather reminiscent of the red violet of the Riviera which would not grow in England. The stems were stout and erect and thus carried the flowers well above the compact plants. It was one of the first to flower, early August in some places, and could flower for ten months in a year, although on Mr Bunyard's nursery, without protection, it only flowered in the spring. It was very highly regarded by James Mayne of Bicton, Budleigh Salterton, Devon, who was thought of as one of the leading non-commercial growers, and it was also well received by other growers. It had reached France by 1889. Large numbers of runners were sold from my Winchester nurseries, the stock having been increased from just one runner. It is probably still in cultivation and has been grown in the USA. Also listed as 'Willisiana'.

'White Czar' (1880). Greenish-white, similar in colour to the hybrid tea rose 'Message' ('White Knight'). Although sometimes regarded as a sport of 'The Czar' to which it was alleged to revert, I have never witnessed any reversion and the shiny foliage is unlike that of 'The Czar'. Not commonly listed.

'**White Imperial**', see 'Imperial White'.

'**White Russian**', see 'Russian'.

'**Willisiana**', see 'Wellsiana'.

'**Wilson**' (1869). Large-flowered pale blue with narrow petals and rather weak stems. Its size and fragrance assured that it would be widely grown; indeed in *Le Jardin*, a French horticultural periodical, a contributor wrote in 1902 that it was one of the main sources of revenue in the Mediterranean region, and in *Gardeners Chronicle* dated 12 April in the same year, it was stated that in France 'no one orders violets, they call them Wilsons'. It was finally superseded by its seedling 'Luxonne'. 'Wilson' is of particular interest as together with 'The Czar', it was the violet most used by Armand Millet for hybridizing (see Chapter 7) and was the parent of several famous cultivars. There is some doubt as to the origin of 'Wilson'; it is generally regarded as a form of *Viola suavis* and this may be the cause of it allegedly not standing up to very cold weather, such as in the Paris area, and thus never being grown in Britain to any appreciable extent. There is one reference to it surviving a sudden frost of 20°C (68°F) but it was protected by snow. There are two accounts of how it reached France; in the French gardening periodical *L'Horticulteur Français* in 1872, it was stated to have been discovered in the ruins of the citadel of Oran in Algeria by M. Ramel, while Edward A. Bunyard stated that it had been discovered by M. Lavallée in Turkey.[12] A. M. Dellor is supposed to have received plants of 'Wilson' from one or both sources and began growing it at Hyères.

'**Windward**' (Windward Violet Nurseries, 1945; 'Lianne' sport). Unusual pale reddish-amethyst 72B. Long stems. Good perfume. Parentage provided by Mrs Grace L. Zambra in an article published in *Amateur Gardening*, issue dated 2 January 1951.

'**Winter Gem**' Listed as a new violet by William Henry Maule of Philadelphia, in 1907. Very large, rich, dark purple flowers on long stems produced freely. Fine perfume. It was believed to be the best of all.

'**Wismar**' (Otto von Mann, Leipzig, Germany, 1895). Large white flowers streaked with lilac.

'**Wren's Pink**' (John Whittlesey, California, USA). Soft shade of pink with delicate perfume and compact habit.

'**Yellow Queen**', see 'Sulfurea'.

'**Yellowette**', see 'Sulfurea'.

'**Yvonne**' (McLeod, NSW, Australia; 'John Raddenbury' seedling). Large blue flowers with a pale pink sheen. Long-stemmed and fragrant.

'**Zariza**' (Germany, *c.*1925; raised from Italian seed). Introduced in the USA by Peter Henderson & Co. of New York. Delicate rose-pink flowers larger than those of 'The Czar' on 20-cm (8-in) stems.

Although all the preceding cultivars have unvariegated foliage, a very few single violets (but no hardy doubles or Parmas) with variegated foliage have been introduced. It is very doubtful whether any of these remain in cultivation. However, there is no reason why variegated-foliage forms should not reappear. Indeed I observed a silver-edged leaf on one of my plants of 'Pamela Zambra' in 1973 and 'Reine des Agenais' appeared in France more recently. Other discoveries include violets with silver edging to leaves only early in the year, and violets with golden leaves.

One of the problems commonly associated with any plant having variegated leaves is the possibility that it will in part revert to the normal green foliage. The reverted portion if not promptly removed will tend to smother the variegated section of the plant due to the green leaves containing more chlorophyll and thus being able to photosynthesize more effectively, so eventually depriving the variegated section of both light and food. Mrs Grace L. Zambra has written that 'Armandine Millet' is not a true cultivar, but as she did not list any other variegated cultivars, the presumption is that she had acquired a reverted stock of that cultivar and it would have been interesting if she had let her readers know to which other violet she considered it identical.

SCENTED SINGLE VIOLETS WITH VARIEGATED LEAVES

'Albo-Marginata' (1871). Silver-edged leaves and dark blue flowers. Listed for more than 20 years, sometimes under the name 'Marginata Alba'.

'Armandine Millet' (Millet, France, 1878; chance seedling). FCC, FCHS 1880. Grown for more than 40 years. It was originally described as having yellow or white variegations, although the plants grown at The Violet Nurseries, Henfield, Sussex, were described as being silver-edged. Some yellow variegations tend to fade to silver with age. The flowers were dark blue and freely produced.

'The Czar Variegated' (1898). Variegated form of 'The Czar'. Purple flowers. Listed for about ten years.

'Marie Guérin' (Forgeot, Paris, c.1880). Raised from seed of unknown parentage. Golden striped foliage.

'Reine des Agenais' (Barandou, France).

'Tigrée Or' (1903). Golden variegated foliage. Dark blue flowers.

NOTES

1. Derek Tangye, *Somewhere a Cat is Waiting* (Michael Joseph, 1977).

2. *The Garden* (17 March 1894).

3. N. Coon and G. Giffen, *The Complete Book of Violets* (Barnes, South Brunswick and New York, 1977).

4. George Jones, *Growing Together: a Gardening History of Geelong* (Australia, 1984).

5. Roy Genders, *Collecting Antique Plants; The History and Culture of the Old Florists Flowers* (Pelham Books, 1971).

6. E. J. Perfect, RHS Journal, October 1965.

7. Armand Millet, *Les Violettes: leurs origins, leurs cultures* (Octave Doin et Libraire Agricole, Paris, 1898). (English translation is now available: see Bibliography.)

8. Edward A. Bunyard, *The New Flora and Silva* (1932).

9. Graham Stuart Thomas, *Colour in the Winter Garden* (Phoenix House, 1957).

10. A. T. Johnson, *A Garden in Wales* (Arnold, 1927).

11. A. T. Johnson, *The Mill Garden* (Collingridge, 1950).

12. Edward A. Bunyard, op cit.

3

SCENTED DOUBLE VIOLETS

(HARDY)

Hardy double violets are a development from the single-flowered form and have been grown for centuries. However, as with other types of violet, it was in the nineteenth century that the range available was considerably improved and widened. The first of the new cultivars was discovered in 1826 or 1827 by M. Bruneau, an amateur gardener living near Paris. 'La Violette de Bruneau' was no larger than the doubles existing hitherto, but it attracted considerable interest as it was the first double to have multi-coloured flowers, the outer petals being deep violet-purple while the inner ones were pale violet-blue, striped with rose. It has already been mentioned that the so-called perpetual single-flowered violet, 'La Violette des Quatre Saisons' became widely grown in France towards the middle of the nineteenth century and that it gave rise to other forms differing in colour, size or freedom and continuity of flowering. One of these was 'La Violette de Champlatreux', supposedly the result of a cross with the wild white single violet, *Viola odorata alba*. This seedling had double white flowers and inherited the perpetual flowering characteristic of 'La Violette des Quatre Saisons' but neither this nor a very similar violet known as 'La Violette des Quatre Saisons à Fleurs Blanches Doubles', seems to have been widely grown, even in France.

For many years, in addition to being planted in borders, hardy double violets were grown in pots and trained to form various shapes. This old skill dated back to at least 1730 in France when it was included in an anonymous appendix (as emphasised by E.J. Perfect in notes with his translation of Armand Millets *Les Violettes*) to La Quintinye's *Instructions sur le Jardinage*, and it reached the height of its popularity in Britain in the mid-nineteenth century. A contemporary account appeared in 1879 in *A Plain Guide to Good Gardening* by Samuel Wood:

'The tree violet is obtained by training a double Russian violet to what is wanted. First select some good healthy long runners in the month of May; cut them off the old stool, and as long as is necessary, trim and plant them in good soil on a south side, and give them a good soaking with water. Plant the whole length of the cutting within one and a half inches [3.75 cm] of the earth. Let the soil be fine and deep, and plant six inches [15 cm] asunder. Keep the young plants clear of runners and encourage the leaders as much as possible; set, if you have one, a hand light over them, they will strike without, but slower. The young plants may remain till September then take them up and pot them into six inch [15 cm] pots using good maiden loam and leaf mould, or else pulverized stable dung, such as old cucumber bed etc. Previously to potting, trim everything clean off the stem to the root; reserve the leader till it has attained the desired height, which should not exceed 15 to 18 inches [38–45 cm] ; then nip the point of the leader out, the tree will then be formed, and should be tied up to a good stick. It will take, at the least, two years to obtain a good plant: it will then be a plant that, with care, will last for years; but, to maintain vigour, feeding must be resorted to.'

Mature trees would sometimes be trained into shapes such as that of an umbrella. The above account provides an answer to Eugene S. Delamer, who wrote at about that time:

> 'The tree violet is regarded as a woody-stemmed species from the Canaries but it may be questioned whether its erect character be not as much due to artificial circumstances as the shrub-like shape of the Tree Mignonette, which is nothing more but the result of training an upright stem to a stick and pinching off the lower shoots.'

It was certainly rather surprising, in view of the amount of time and labour that was necessary to persuade the violets to form into trees, that anyone should regard tree violets as a separate species; nevertheless such was the case, although not everyone thought of its place of origin as the Canary Isles, and it was given the specific name *Viola arborea* or *V. arborescens* (the latter name is now used for a distinct European wild violet).

The Royal Horticultural Society awarded a Certificate of Merit to Messrs Hayes of Lower Edmonton, Middlesex, England, for 'two nicely managed plants of tree violets' at its meeting on 1 April 1851, and tree violets, not always double-flowered, were produced by several nurseries in Britain and sold at the markets. James Backhouse and Son of York, in their 1867 catalogue, offered *Viola arborea* (the 'Chinese Tree Violet') at one shilling [five pence] each but, grown as trees with stems five to ten years old, the price asked was from five shillings [25 pence] to two guineas [£2.10 each]. While *V. arborea* continued to be offered until 1883 as plants by that nursery, trees were not again listed, so that may have been about the time when their popularity waned in the UK, many years before they lost favour in Europe.

It was not surprising in view of the specific status given to tree violets that the next important development to be introduced was regarded as a form of the tree violet, the *Viola arborea* 'Brandyana', introduced in 1863 and raised by C. Brandy, another French amateur gardener, who lived in Mars, Sarthe. This cultivar resembled 'Bruneau' except that the outer petals as well as the inner ones were also variegated. This cultivar was listed by several British nurseries, often incorrectly named 'Blandyana'. As early as 1881, the Reverend Rawson, Vicar of Bromley, Kent, England, a leading amateur violet grower, wrote that 'it lost its stripes constantly'; nevertheless, for many years it remained listed by British nurseries.

Two important British hardy doubles were introduced in the 1860s; the first of these was 'Queen of Violets' released in 1866, being described by Dillistone and Woodthorp of Sturmer, Suffolk and Braintree, Essex, England, as 'the most lovely of all violets, no garden or conservatory can be complete without it'. They claimed that they 'received hundreds of flattering testimonials from all parts of the country, speaking in the highest terms of this variety'. The colour of this cultivar was similar to that of *Viola odorata alba*, the buds being purple and the flowers when fully open being white, or almost white. The second cultivar, 'King of Violets', was introduced in the following year, being described as an improvement on the old double purple cultivar. Both these cultivars were grown in the USA and Canada, as well as Europe.

'Queen of Violets' had been recommended for use in conservatories and as the use of the hardy double cultivars as trees waned, so they increasingly were used to extend the colour range of the tender Parma violets grown in pots under glass (indeed even the single cultivar 'The Czar' was being used to provide a purple-coloured potted violet at Longford Castle, Salisbury, Wiltshire in 1881). The next hardy double to be introduced, 'Belle de Châtenay', a seedling of 'The Czar' raised by L. Paillet in France, was seized on at once for flowering in pots under glass. Rather similar to 'Queen of Violets', the mauve buds and large white flowers, occasionally flecked with mauve-carmine, especially when grown in the open, the best flowers of this cultivar were described as being as large as shillings (old 5p pieces) and were recommended for use in buttonholes. Unfortunately, particularly under glass, a high proportion of the flowers were malformed and thus fell far short of the raiser's perhaps biased statement that it was the most beautiful of all violets. The introduction of further colour forms of the Parma violet, notably 'Swanley White' in 1884, soon ended the use of hardy doubles under glass, as the former had a longer flowering season, often longer stems and were generally more reliable under this type of culture.

'Patrie', another purple or Chinese blue cultivar, was also introduced in 1877 and differed from the other cultivars of similar coloration by having slight red streaks near to the centre of the flower. However, its main attraction was its approach to perpetual flowering. In 1890 R. W. Beachey wrote that at his nursery at Kingskerswell, Devon, in a damp summer it would flower every month. Messrs Chambers of Westlake Nursery, Spring Grove, Isleworth,

Middlesex, released 'Chambers' Victoria' in 1887, which was claimed to be a cross between 'The Czar' and 'Neapolitan' ('Neapolitan' being the forerunner of the Parma violets) and was awarded the Royal Horticultural Society's First Class Certificate, the first and only hardy double to be so honoured. Despite its alleged parentage it appeared to be fully hardy, so much so in fact that it was regarded by at least one writer as being the same as the older 'King of Violets' and by others as being identical to 'Madame [or Mademoiselle] Berthe Barron', a rather shy-flowering indigo cultivar of almost perfect form.

No new hardy double cultivars of this type have been introduced for about 70 years and many excellent cultivars are probably now extinct; it is difficult to account for this decline, which was roughly parallel in time to the decline of the double primrose and the double auricula, as well as even the Parma violets, unless it was due to a passing dislike of double flowers. Hardy double violets have been criticized for flowering late in the season, after the majority of the singles, but by so doing, additional interest is created towards the end of the violet flowering season. Another criticism is that they do not flower in the autumn and winter, but that is not supported by my observations both in Hampshire and Devon. The cultural treatment required by these violets is identical to that for a single cultivar of average growth; derunnering will be necessary, as with the singles of which they are merely a form, and of course there is no need to provide them with the sort of protection that is vital to the tender double-flowered Parma violets. Thus if single violets thrive in a garden, it can be expected that the hardy doubles will do likewise.

From the mid-1960s until 1980, I believe that my nursery was the only commercial source for the two hardy double cultivars then listed in Britain. Both cultivars were obtained from the Windward Violet Nurseries after Mr Ayres bought Windward from the Zambras. 'Double Rose' is a vigorous, long-stemmed, lavender-rose violet with rather obscure origins. This may be 'Double Rose de Bruant', which was mentioned in France in the 1880s and was probably an improved form of the original 'Double Rose' that dates back to at least Tudor times. The second cultivar is 'Comte de Chambord' which was first listed in England in 1901; this has flowers similar in colour to 'Belle de Châtenay' except that the fully open flowers are off-white instead of pure white and are of better quality, and the colour of the flower buds is also different. Both these surviving cultivars are free-flowering and the blooms are carried on long stems, ideal for picking. A double indigo cultivar thought by the Windward Violet Nurseries to be 'King of Violets' also exists and although it nearly became extinct in Britain, it should not have been in this parlous position as it is an easy grower and very free-flowering. The double form of the flowers appears to give this cultivar an extra intensity when compared with similar-coloured singles. The form of the flowers may also suggest that it is a more recent introduction than 'King of Violets'. There is a possibility that

'Queen of Violets' still survives in Britain (I obtained a violet with this name from Northern Ireland) as well as another double white cultivar which I obtained as 'Blanche de Chevreuse'. Both these acquisitions were distinct from the hardy doubles I was already growing. Nevertheless completely distinct and very choice cultivars have been lost, including a pale blue cultivar mentioned by the compilers of the old herbals and the old double red (probably magenta), neither of which were adequately replaced by later cultivars.

The hardy doubles are much easier to grow than the Parma cultivars and, despite lacking their unique perfume, are as sweetly scented as the majority of the singles. The rescue from extinction of at least some of these cultivars may be the most tangible result to date of the revival of interest in the scented violet. However, as with the singles, one is always left with the thought that in many gardens, rare violets still survive and that their identity, and thus their importance and value, is completely unknown to their present owners.

Since 1980, rediscoveries among this class of violet demonstrate how violet growers in several countries are working together. Cultivars at present known as 'Mme Dumas' and 'Le Gresley' from France and Ontario, Canada respectively have come to the attention of violet enthusiasts. 'Jazz' and 'King of Violets' have remained in Australian plant lists over many years and John Whittlesey in California has probably saved 'Double Russian' from extinction by building up a stock of plants from just one surviving plant. I use the word 'probably' not to lessen his achievement but because, as I mentioned earlier, there is always the possibility of 'lost' cultivars and indeed additional stocks of 'found' cultivars surviving and awaiting rediscovery.

CULTIVARS OF SCENTED DOUBLE VIOLETS (HARDY)

'**Alba Compacta**' (1870). White.

'**Alba Fragrantissima Plena**' (Belgium, 1869). White. Raised from seed, near Ghent.

'**Alba Plena de Chevreuse**' (France, 1890). Rose buds opening to white flowers. Also listed as 'Blanche de Chevreuse'.

'**Belle de Châtenay**' (L. Paillet, Châtenay-les-Sceaux, France, 1877; seedling from 'The Czar'). Purple buds opening to white flowers.

'**Belle de Châtenay Caerulea Plena**' (1869). Claimed to be a large-flowered deep blue seedling of 'Belle de Châtenay'.

'**Blanche de Chevennes**' (1908). White. Possibly a synonym of 'Alba Plena de Chevreuse'.

'**Blanche de Chevreuse**', see 'Alba Plena de Chevreuse'.

'**Blandyana**', see 'Brandyana'.

'**Brandyana**' (Brandy, France, 1863). Deep blue ground, striped with rose. Rather short stems. Grown widely in Britain and France. In 1872 the journal of the Hamburg Horticultural Society recorded that it was grown well in that part of Germany. Some years later in the Bunyard catalogue it was graphically described 'true and very scarce, but being the most distinct cultivar, it is remarkable it should be so; the flowers are intense dark purple, with a well-defined rosy pink stripe down each petal which makes it a gem and a variety not to be easily forgotten'. Also listed as 'Brandyanum', 'Blandyana' and 'Blandyanum'.

'Bruneau' (Bruneau, France, 1826). Similar to 'Brandyana' except that the rosy stripes are present only on the inner petals. Also listed as 'Brunoni' and 'Bruneautiana'.

'Cape Cod Violet', see 'Double Russian'.

'Chambers' Victoria' (Chambers, 1880; 'The Czar' x 'Neapolitan'). FCC, RHS, 1887. Deep blue. Some growers have considered this to be a new name for 'King of Violets', others have thought it to be identical to 'Madame Berthe Barron'.

'Champlatreux' (Mabire, France 1848; 'Quatre Saisons' x *Viola odorata alba*). White flowers with the extended flowering season of 'Quatre Saisons'.

'Comte de Chambord' (1895). Purple buds opening to large off-white flowers. Mrs Grace L. Zambra wrote that at the Windward Violet Nurseries it gave only 'a stray bloom or two in the autumn', but both in Winchester and Honiton it flowered steadily from autumn onwards. Also listed as 'Comte de Chambaud'.

'Deutsche Kaiserin' (1890). Dark blue.

'Double Blue'. A violet listed under this name by the Windward Violet Nurseries was thought to be 'King of Violets'. The flower is almost certainly too refined to be that cultivar. It could possibly be the old double blue that has been grown for centuries or more likely one of the later cultivars. A feature of the Windward 'Double Blue' was the attractive appearance of the plants even when not flowering as they seemed ideal for edging a flower bed.

'Double Purple'. A very old form which was used for many years as a tree violet and consequently was often listed as *Viola arborea*. Deep purple. 'Scotch' and *V. odorata plena* may be synonymous.

'Double Red'. The centuries-old red or copper cultivar, which Mr Lee compared to a double red hepatica (another rare plant). Also listed as 'Rubra Plena', 'Rubra Pleno' and 'Double Red Russian'. This cultivar was notable for its long flowering season from September to March.

'Double Rose'. A double rose violet has also been grown for centuries. Whether the one still in cultivation is the original is not known. A possibly improved form, 'Double Rose de Bruant', appeared in about 1889. The form obtained from the Windward Violet Nurseries as 'Double Rose' in the early 1960s, and which over the years I supplied by mail order, had beautiful lavender-rose 72B buds and flowers on long stems quite suitable for cutting.

Seed and seedlings were produced which in my experience were always the
same as the parent.

'**Double Russian**' (1886). Very dark bluish-purple 9A (but darker). It tended to
replace the old 'Double Purple' for use as a tree violet. It was still listed in
the 1930s in the UK, but much more recently in the USA where it is
sometimes called the 'Cape Cod Violet'.

'**Double White**'. Again, centuries old. One of the most famous of all violets.
Francis Bacon referred to it as the most sweetly scented plant in all the
garden. G. A. Stevens described it in 1938 as the 'hardiest violet'.[1]

'**Elegantissima Plena**' (1886). Blue. Form of flower similar to 'Patrie'.

'**Empress**' (Cannell). Purple.

'**Forncett Mavis**' (Four Seasons Nursery, Norfolk, 2001; chance seedling).
Lilac.

'**French Grey**', see 'Comte de Chambord'.

'**Imperial**'. Deep blue with slight scent. There is also a Parma cultivar with this
name.

'**James Watt**'(1899). Purple.

'**Jazz**' (Australia). Buds and flowers are both purple and white. Lovely
perfume.

'**King of Violets**' (1866). Deep purplish-blue. A violet with this name and
description has been grown extensively in Australia in recent years.

'**Langport Blue**' (1896). Deep blue.

'**La Parisienne**'. Regarded as synonymous with 'Patrie'. 'La Belle Parisienne'
has been listed as a Parma cultivar.

'**Le Gresley**'. This cultivar is known to have been brought to Canada probably
from the North of England and has been grown there for a minimum of
almost 150 years. Plants were reintroduced to the UK in 1997 and is in
cultivation at C. W. Groves and Son at Bridport, Dorset.

'**Louise Barron**' (France, 1904). Deep blue.

'**Mme Berthe Barron**' (France, 1885). Indigo. Also listed as 'Mlle Berthe
Barron'.

'**Mme Dumas**'. An old cultivar from the garden of Mme Dumas in Tarn-en-
Garonne, France, given to Nathalie Casbas who introduced it in 1982. A
very hardy double blue violet.

'**Patrie**' (France, 1870). Thought to be a double form of the wild violet of the
Crimea, this cultivar may have come from Asia Minor. Purplish-blue
flowers with reddish streaks. Although the flowering season was from
September to April, in ideal conditions flowers have been found during
every month of the year.

'**Princess Elizabeth**' (1871). Large white.

'**Princess Irene**' (i) (1925). Dark blue cultivar grown in France. (ii) Thought by
Mrs Grace L. Zambra to be identical to 'Double Rose'.

'**Purple King**'. Blackish-purple.

'**Queen of Violets**' (1865). Rose-pink buds opening to white flowers.

'**Queen of Violets Caerulea Plena**' (1886). Supposed to be a blue form of the above cultivar.

'**Rose Double**', see 'Double Rose'.

'**Rose Double de Bruant**', see 'Double Rose'.

'**Scotch**' (1865). Blue. Possibly synonymous with 'Double Purple'.

NOTE

1. G. A. Stevens, *Garden Flowers in Colour* (Macmillan, 1938).

4
SCENTED
SEMI-DOUBLE VIOLETS

(HARDY)

Early last century, another type of hardy double violet appeared. This was not a development of the ordinary singles as the previously described cultivars had been, but of the giant singles which had only recently been introduced and which had already become grown extensively. The first of these new cultivars, often called semi-doubles or double singles, was introduced by Vilmorin in France in 1905. This cultivar had large rounded petals, typical of the best of the giant singles, with an additional central rosette or eye composed of small orange or white petalloids. It was aptly named 'Cyclope' after the race of one-eyed giants who in Greek mythology were supposed to have inhabited Sicily. Although 'Cyclope' was grown quite widely in Britain, it failed to achieve much popularity.

Some years later, a similar violet was introduced by J. J. Kettle's Violet Farm at Corfe Mullen in Dorset. Mr Kettle recorded that it was a seedling of the blue single cultivar 'John Raddenbury' which had been popularized there as a market cut flower. Prior to 1913 Mr Kettle had always found that the seedlings produced by that cultivar were identical to the parent, but in that year seed was sown that had resulted from 'John Raddenbury' flowers being pollinated with 'Cyclope' pollen, by ants.

When the resultant seedlings flowered, Mr Kettle noted that 20 per cent were deeper in colour than 'John Raddenbury'. One seedling proved worthy of special attention; indeed Mr Kettle regarded it as the most advanced form of violet flower he had yet seen and this he named 'Mrs David Lloyd George' after the wife of the leader of the Liberal Party and Prime Minister from 1916 to 1922. This cultivar surpassed 'Cyclope' by having a larger eye with multi-coloured petalloids, and it proved to be much more popular with the florists, so much so that two acres were planted in an attempt to meet the demand. It received the Royal Horticultural Society's Award of Merit in 1918 and a Gold Medal at the 1925 New York flower show. There had been some controversy as to whether this violet was merely 'Cyclope' reintroduced under another name, but Mr Kettle's subsequent introductions of a similar type would seem to validate his description of how it originated. The authors of *The Complete*

Book of Violets (1977) described it as a seedling of 'Princesse de Galles';[1] I wrote in 1980 that it would have been interesting to know if there was a sound basis for their disregarding the account by Mr Kettle, which was published in the *Journal of the Royal Horticultural Society* in 1918, but as far as I am aware, there was no response.

Two years after 'Mrs David Lloyd George' was raised, another seedling of this type was discovered at Corfe Mullen, this time among plants of 'Princesse de Galles'. The development from the giant singles first noted in 'Cyclope', and later seen in a more refined state in 'Mrs David Lloyd George', was taken even further as this new cultivar, named 'Princess Mary', had instead of a rosette, a second row of violet-blue petals within the outer row. This cultivar was described by one leading nursery as the best violet ever introduced, and Nelson Coon, the American horticultural writer, who was at that time principal of the Rhinebeck Floral Company, wrote that Mr Kettle regarded this cultivar as the triumph of his years of work with the violet. The Royal Horticultural Society bestowed the Award of Merit on it in 1924. Frederick E. Dillistone wrote a year or two later that everyone who had seen 'Princess Mary' flowering in the autumn without protection in his nursery at Sturmer in Suffolk, was captivated by it and he predicted that it would have a big future.[2]

Mr Kettle exhibited in 1928 another cultivar of this type, which has been described variously as outstanding and glorious, and by Messrs H. R. Jones and Son, who purchased the Violet Farm after Mr Kettle's death in 1933, as their most admired violet. This was 'Countess of Shaftesbury', also found among plants of 'Princesse de Galles'. The new cultivar differed in that the flowers, although still having violet-blue outer petals, had in addition a centre composed of fairly small rose-pink petals and the two colours harmonized in a most delightful manner.

Further seedlings of the same type were raised from deliberate crosses, and H. W. Abbiss, successively Horticultural Superintendent of Devonshire and Cornwall, the leading English counties where violets for cut flowers are grown, had obviously seen or received information about these, as he wrote that several good semi-doubles had been raised at Corfe Mullen that would appeal to commercial growers.[3] Regrettably, this programme of hybridization seems to have ended with Mr Kettle's death and even the later introductions and new seedlings, which were being acclaimed by Frederick E. Dillistone,[4] were not proceeded with.

The sensational violets raised at Corfe Mullen were strongly fragrant, the perfume being reminiscent of wild violets rather than the giant singles, and they possessed strong, long stems and large, almost circular, leaves identical to those of the giant singles such as 'Askania' and 'Princesse de Galles'. The long-lasting flowers (the rosettes tended to prevent the outer petals from closing) and unfading colours were also requisites of good market violets, so it was not surprising that when first introduced, the flowers of 'Mrs David Lloyd George' fetched twice as much on the markets than had the previous bestsellers, 'La France' and 'Princesses de Galles'. Both 'Mrs David Lloyd George' and 'Princess Mary' were still being recommended by the Ministry of Agriculture in 1965 as suitable cut-flower cultivars, and 'Countess of Shaftesbury' was also eminently suitable for that purpose. Mr Kettle's violets were also popular for planting in private gardens, because of their large, unusual flowers and very strong, sweet perfume.

In the 1980 edition of this book I wrote, regrettably, that none of these violets were readily obtainable in Britain. 'Mrs David Lloyd George' was still listed by at least one nursery in the USA in 1973 and 'Princess Mary' still survived in very small numbers in Britain, as well as probably in the USA. In contrast, in the 1920s, in the USA alone, one nursery firm, the Rhinebeck Floral Company, was growing 5,000 plants of these two violets. I hoped that 'Countess of Shaftesbury' might have been found and that these violets could be conserved as a living memorial both to their raiser and to the Violet Farm he founded, which ceased trading in 1968.

I also mentioned that the pioneer cultivar 'Cyclope' was unobtainable, as was a large semi-double white cultivar, 'Reine des Blanches'. The latter first appeared in the 1920s and was tried out in Devon where it was found to be very shy-flowering. All these semi-doubles require the same treatment as the giant singles and should therefore be quite easy to grow. Their almost total disappearance at that time owed more to accidents of history than to any failing on their part. In 1980, I noted that there was a tendency among plants I grew of 'Mrs David Lloyd George' to evolve into a form very similar or possibly identical to 'Countess of Shaftesbury'. Kerry Carman in New Zealand has observed variation among 'Mrs David Lloyd George' flowers and recorded the occurrence in a watercolour painting (see bibliography).

In 2003, small quantities of plants are being produced and listed as 'Countess of Shaftesbury', 'Cyclope' and 'Mrs David Lloyd George'. John Whittlesey rediscovered 'Countess of Shaftesbury' in California and plants of these cultivars have survived in Australia and New Zealand and provide another example of enthusiasts working together. I believe the search for plants of 'Princess Mary' is still in progress.

CULTIVARS OF SCENTED SEMI-DOUBLE VIOLETS (HARDY)
'Countess of Shaftesbury' (Kettle, 1928; 'Princesse de Galles' seedling). Mid-blue outer petals with rose-pink rosette. Long stems, ideal for picking. One of the most beautiful violets in cultivation in recent years. Listed in the early 1960s and after years of absence, these plants are again available in limited quantities.
'Cyclope' (Vilmorin, France, 1905; possibly from 'Gloire de Bourg-la-Reine').

Blue petals with a white and orange rosette centre. Long stems. Grown rarely or not at all in the UK for many years but now obtainable again.

'**Duchess of Sutherland**'. Mentioned as being in this category in horticultural writing of the 1950s.

'**Lady Lloyd George**', see 'Mrs David Lloyd George'.

'**Mrs David Lloyd George**' (Kettle, 1915; 'John Raddenbury' x 'Cyclope'). AM, RHS, 1918. Gold Medal, New York Flower Show, 1925. Blue outer petals with a large multi-coloured rosette. Listed in Britain in the 1960s and in the USA in 1973. Probably obtainable again in the UK after many years' absence. MRCF.

'**Princess Mary**' (Kettle, 1917; 'Princesse de Galles' seedling). AM, RHS, 1924. Gold Medal, New York Flower Show, 1928. Giant bluish-violet flowers composed of two rows of petals. Listed in the early 1960s in Britain. One of the most sought-after of the 'lost' violets. MRCF.

'**Reine des Blanches**' (1921). White.

NOTES

1. N. Coon and G. Giffen, *The Complete Book of Violets* (A.S. Barnes, South Brunswick and New York, 1977).

2. Frederick E. Dillistone, *Violet Culture for Pleasure and Profit* (Ernest Benn, 1926).

3. H. W. Abbiss, *Commercial Violet Production* (Cornwall County Education Committee, 1938).

4. Frederick E. Dillistone, *Violet Culture for Pleasure and Profit*, 2nd edn (Ernest Benn, 1933).

Viola hederacea,
V. hederacea 'Blue Baby'

V. sieberiana,
V. verecunda var
yakusimana,
V. cunninghami

V. langsdorffii
(syn V. kamtschadalorum)

V. dissecta f. eizanensis
alba

V. calaminaria

V. elatior

V. pubescens
var eriocarpa

V. canadensis

V. sororia rubra (syns V.
cucullata rubra, V. obliqua
rubra), V. s. 'Freckles' and
'Freckles' Blue Form

V. sororia 'White Ladies'

V. s. 'Gloriole'

V. 'Delmonden'

V. priceana and
V. pedatifida

V. pedata

V. 'Sylvia Hart'
(*V. selkirkiii*)

V. grypocera exilis
(syn *V. Koreana)*

Lee violets: H1

H10

H13

H15

H16

H19

H2

H21

H23

H24

H25

H2A

H3 (1)

H3(2)

H3D

H3A

H3B

H3E

H4

H5

H7

H8E

H8E(1)

H9

H9B

H9B

H9C

H9C

'Josephine'

'Katja'

'Lady Hume Campbell'

'Lady Jane'

'Mignonette'

Orchid Pink

cultivar often mistakenly identified as 'Pamela Zambra'

'Köningin Charlotte'

'Köningin Charlotte'

'Köningin Charlotte'

'Red Charm'

'Rosanna'

'Rosine'

'St Helena'

Queensland form

'Lavender Lady'

'Kaiserin Augusta'

'Reid's Crimson Carpet'

'The Czar'

Queensland form

Lee violet

'Columbine'

'Cordelia'

Tregaskus form

Viola biflora

Viola selkirkii

'Yvonne Matthews'

'Yvonne Matthews'

KEY TO CULTIVARS

1 'Köningin Charlotte'
2 'Columbine'
3 'Mignonette'
4 'Cordelia'
5 'Crepuscule'
6 'Katja'
7 'Bournemouth Gem'
8 'Baroness Rothschild'
9 'Sisters'
10 'Yvonne Matthews'
11 'Mother's Day'
12 'Red Charm'

Viola odorata (© J. Sarsby)

'Irish Elegance' (© C. Matthews)

'Marie Louise' and 'Duchess de Parme' (© C. Matthews)

'Ash Vale Blue' (© Clive Groves)

'Becky Groves' (© Clive Groves)

'Charles William Groves' (© Clive Groves)

'Columbine' (© Clive Groves)

'Crepuscule' (© Clive Groves)

'Diana Groves' (© Clive Groves)

'Elsie Coombs' (© Clive Groves)

'Clive Groves' (© Clive Groves)

'Gloire de Verdun' (© Clive Groves)

'Lydia Groves' (© Clive Groves)

'Lady Jane' (© Clive Groves)

'Opera' (© Clive Groves)

'Köningin Charlotte' (© Clive Groves)

'Parme de Toulouse' (© J. Sarsby)

'Josephine' (© Clive Groves)

'Bournemouth Gem' (© J. Sarsby)

'Mrs R Barton' (© J. Sarsby)

'Reid's Crimson Carpet' (© J. Sarsby)

'St Helena' (© J. Sarsby)

'Governor Herrick' (© J. Sarsby)

Hardy double white (© J. Sarsby)

Viola priceana (the Confederate violet) (© J. Sarsby)

Double Rose (hardy double) (© J. Sarsby)

'Princess Diana' (© J. Sarsby)

'Luxonne' (© C. Matthews)

Mixed violets with cultivars 'The Czar', 'Baronne Alice de Rothschild' and Cornish white
(© C. Matthews)

'Norah Church' (© C. Matthews)

'Köningin Charlotte' (© C. Matthews)

'The Czar' (© C. Matthews)

'Perle Rose' (© C. Matthews)

Mixed violets with 'Irish Elegance', 'Norah Church', 'Cornish White', 'The Czar', 'Perle Rose', 'Mrs R Barton', 'Opera', 'Bournemouth Gem' and 'Princess Diana' (© C. Matthews)

44 Mixed violets with 'Luxonne', 'John Raddenbury', 'Elsie Coombs' and 'Amiral Avellan'.
(© C. Matthews)

Viola odorata at the NCCPG National Collection (© C. Matthews)

'Amiral Avellan' (© C. Matthews)

Commercial boxed violets, 'Governor Herrick', exhibited by West Combe Gardens at the Penzance Show, 2000 (© C. Matthews)

Yellow-leaved violet from Torbay. The leaves turn green later in the year.
(© C. Matthews)

Violets in pots (© C. Matthews)

'Neapolitan' (© C. Matthews)

Lee violet H3E (© C. Matthews)

The only surviving image of Clevedon violets (Jean Canter)

Planting violets at Isaac House & Son, 1907
(© The estate of H.H Crane, *The Book of The Pansy, Viola, Violet*, Bodley Head)

5
SCENTED PARMA VIOLETS

(TENDER)

These cultivars, perhaps the most beautiful and certainly the most challenging of the scented violets, have been grown in the UK for more than 180 years. In ideal conditions they will flower freely from autumn until May, and the flowers possess a delightful fragrance reminiscent of ordinary sweet violet perfume mixed with that of wallflowers. Hardy only in the mildest parts of the British Isles, these violets have small, pointed, glossy leaves and a compact habit as long runners are not produced by the majority of Parma cultivars. The habit is rather similar to the single cultivars 'Lianne' and 'La Violette des Quatre Saisons'. It has been suggested that the characteristics that distinguish Parma violets from the other forms of *Viola odorata*, both single and double, are sufficient to show that they are derived from another fragrant *Viola* species rather than from *V. odorata*. Possible confirmation that they should be a distinct species is that none have been discovered growing wild in the UK where *V. odorata* is a native species.

The origin of these violets is still obscure although all the cultivars grown here were either obtained from the Italian peninsula or were evolved from stock that had been imported from there. Their homeland traditionally has been considered to be Asia Minor or the Levant, and if so they could have been brought to Europe by Genoese or Venetian merchants. At least one Parma violet was being grown in the gardens of the Empress Josephine of France at Malmaison, and at the latest it must have reached the UK soon after: in 1820 Isaac Oldaker, gardener to Czar Alexander I of Russia, described to The Horticultural Society how he had cultivated 300 plants of this violet in pots for his late employer, Sir Joseph Banks, who for over 40 years had been President of the Royal Society and an ardent horticulturist. The violets had been grown at Spring Grove, Isleworth, from 1816 to 1819.

This violet was the Neapolitan violet or *Viola odorata pallida plena* (sometimes *V. suavis pallida plena italica*) which remained in cultivation until quite recent years, both in Britain and the USA. In France it was called 'La Violette de Parme' or 'La Violette de Naples' and, perhaps surprisingly in view of the latter, it was called the 'Portuguese Violet' in Naples. 'Neapolitan' remained for about 50 years the only violet of this type to be grown in Britain and when variants did occur, they were referred to as forms of the Neapolitan violet. However, as the years passed, the term 'Parma violets' slowly replaced

'Neapolitan violets' here, although the original form continued to be known as the Neapolitan violet. The differing names serve to confuse the history of these violets and, to make matters worse, identification of the various forms that were subsequently introduced has proved to be even more difficult than with other types of violet. Also, several of them have been reintroduced under other names and the differences between genuinely distinct cultivars can be very small.

The flowers of 'Neapolitan' were carried on weaker stems than many of the later introductions and were pale lavender in colour. All the Parma violets had white centres, of somewhat variable size, and all those mentioned here had double flowers (for single-flowered Parmas, see later in this chapter). This violet was usually regarded as sterile with all the colour variants that occurred being mutations (sports) from the original type, either found in cultivation or collected from the wild. However, at least two cultivars, 'Madame Millet' and 'Colcronan hybrid', were described as being seedlings, while as mentioned in Chapter 3, Messrs Chambers of Isleworth stated that their award-winning hardy double, 'Chambers' Victoria', was the result of a cross between 'The Czar' and 'Neapolitan'. Another view was that most, although not quite all, of the mutations were the result of the original type reacting to differing cultural conditions, and were therefore likely to change back at any time, as opposed to a true mutation which would only rarely revert. It is worth noting that several violets, not all being Parmas, can be affected by differing conditions, to the extent that the degree of red in the coloration can be lessened or intensified, thus removing or producing lilac or carmine highlights.

During the 1860s, at least four colour variations were recorded. The first of these was 'Parmaensis Flore Plena' with white flowers striped with rose. It came to Britain from France and was still being listed 40 years later. 'Marie Louise', probably after the Austrian archduchess Maria Louisa, the second wife of the Emperor Napoleon I of France, was introduced from Heidelburg, Baden (which was soon to be incorporated in the German Empire) in 1865; its flowers were large, strongly scented and deep violet-mauve in colour. Plants were exported to the USA in 1872, and two years later they were being offered for sale there by John Cook of Baltimore, Maryland, and became very popular, being planted on a larger scale than 'Neapolitan'. 'New York', first listed as *Viola odorata pendula* – the 'Weeping Violet of New York', closely resembled 'Marie Louise' in colour except that there were small splashes of red on the deep violet-mauve ground colour, particularly on the inner petals. Both these stocks became mixed, or further mutation occurred, as 'Marie Louise' was often described as having red markings. The fourth cultivar raised in the 1860s, 'Madame Millet', will be mentioned later.

From about 1873, nurseries in England began listing a cultivar named 'de Parme', often in addition to 'Neapolitan', so it was obviously distinct. This was probably the violet that is still grown today as 'Duchesse de Parme'. It had come from Florence in Italy three years earlier, being first mentioned in the horticultural press in November 1870. It had lavender-mauve flowers, a shade deeper than 'Neapolitan', the stems were stronger and the plants more vigorous. For much of the 1970s it was the only Parma violet being sold in the UK.

In 1875 the Parma cultivar 'Lady Hume Campbell' was introduced. It was named after the person who had found it near Milan, in northern Italy, and who had subsequently grown it for several years at Highgrove, Eastcote, Pinner, Middlesex, in England. The flowers were perfectly formed and in colour between 'Duchesse de Parme' and 'Marie Louise'. It was especially of value as it flowered late, into May in cool conditions, and very freely. The flowers were also strongly scented. Hundreds of pots of this violet were sold each year by J. J. Kettle who wrote, after years of experience with the Parmas, that he regarded it as the best for that purpose due to its propensity for having many flowers open at one time, as well as the best Parma for cutting from February onwards. 'Lady Hume Campbell' was regarded as an excellent cultivar for planting in private gardens, too. For instance at Broome Park, Alnwick, northern England, 100 plants yielded between 600 and 1,000 flowers every week throughout the season, picking being undertaken twice weekly. It was imported by H. Huebner of Groton, Massachusetts, in 1892 and its excellent constitution led to its widespread cultivation by cut-flower growers in several states.

Year by year the popularity of these violets steadily increased, indeed it would be difficult to overstate their international appeal. Alphonse Karr wrote: 'Go to the opera and you will see 200 women with bunches of violets in their hands.'[1] Young ladies wore Parma violets on their lapels or muffs[2] and in Florence and Paris, bouquets were made of Parma violets either surrounded by snowdrops, or surrounding a white camellia. In view of this interest it was not surprising that many large nurseries were offering a wide range of cultivars as well as searching for new ones. Henry Cannell's Swanley Nurseries at Swanley, Kent, England, purchased a stock of a unique white-flowered Parma from Conte Savorgnin di Brazza of Sorreschian, near Udine in north-east Italy, then close to the Austro–Hungarian frontier. Cannell named this cultivar 'Swanley White' at the suggestion, he said, of the fuchsia grower, E. Bland. Soon Cannell was exporting it to the USA, where it became widely grown, although never on the scale of the other Parmas because of its colour. Nevertheless, according to a writer in *The Garden and Forest* in 1892, it was highly prized by a few people for evening wear and this fashion is illustrated in Coon and Giffen's *The Complete Book of Violets* (see page 39). It was much more sought-after in Britain as the hardy doubles had proved to be less reliable for flowering under glass than the Parmas, and 'Swanley White' lived up to all expectations. Other growers, notably T. S. Ware of Feltham and Tottenham, England, obtained plants of this cultivar from the Conte di Brazza, despite the undertakings he was alleged to have given Cannell. These new importations were usually under the name 'Comte Brazza's White Neapolitan' or 'Comte Brazza' and it was under the latter of these names that it was awarded the Royal Horticultural Society's First Class Certificate when exhibited by Lord Suffield of Gunton Park, Norwich on 13 November 1883. 'Swanley White' is still grown in the UK as well as in the USA, but in minute numbers compared with the years following its introduction. Nevertheless, its strongly scented, pure white flowers of good form, sometimes with a pale blue tint, always attract attention.

The occurrence of pale blue sports of 'Swanley White' was soon being recorded, one named 'Robert Garrett' in the USA in 1888, another, 'Dowager Lady Williams Wynn' from Llangedwyn, Oswestry, Shropshire, England, in 1900 when it was shown to the Royal Horticultural Society, and there were several more, for instance from Norfolk and Northumberland, but none became widely grown. The probable reason for this was that although attractive, they were found to be identical to 'Neapolitan', from which 'Swanley White' may have been obtained as a sport and to which some plants were reverting. I mentioned in the first edition of this book that if this supposition should be correct and growers of 'Swanley White' were to exercise vigilance, *Pallida plena*, or 'Neapolitan', which might be extinct would be found again and I understand that this has indeed been the origin for at least some of the stocks of 'Neapolitan' now again offered for sale. Such a procedure, though time-consuming is doubly beneficial as it not only recreates a lost cultivar, 'Neapolitan', but it also ensures that the 'Conte di Brazza' (Comte Brazza) plants retain their outstanding beauty.

In the 1880s, another significant addition to the colour range was introduced in the UK and in the USA; this was 'Madame Millet', introduced by Millet et Fils of Bourg-la-Reine near Paris, who have already been mentioned as important raisers of single violets (see also Chapter 7). However, this cultivar was raised by another violet grower in the Paris area, M. Néant of Bièvres, Seine-et-Oise, in 1868. It was thought to be a seedling of 'de Parme' (presumably the cultivar grown here as 'Neapolitan'). 'New York' had shown reddish markings but the new cultivar was at that time the closest approach to a self-red Parma, being variously described as reddish-violet, rose, violet-purple shaded carmine and rosy-lilac shaded carmine. Presumably some at least of these differences were caused, as mentioned earlier in this chapter, by varying cultural conditions. 'Madame Millet' was strongly scented and flowered freely, and was first offered for sale in the USA by John Cook of Baltimore in 1888, when it was described in *Meehan's Monthly* as being an entirely new and unexpected colour. In November 1894 it attracted attention when exhibited by R. W. Beachey at the Torquay Chrysanthemum Show, Devon, England.

During the 1890s, violet cultivation in its traditional centres in Massachusetts and elsewhere in New England became increasingly important, while north of New York City, in an area not previously noted for violet growing, George Saltford planted 800 'Marie Louise'. When these commenced flowering, 85,000 blooms were produced in three months. Saltford continued growing violets with undiminished success and his example, which he was not slow to publicize (see Bibliography), led to further violet nurseries being established there. This was the beginning of the violet industry at Rhinebeck-on-Hudson. By 1906 cultivation had spread around the neighbouring settlements of Barrytown, Rock City and Staatsburg, as well as the larger towns of Poughkeepsie and Red Hook, and Rhinebeck had become the centre of the most important violet-growing area in the USA. In all, there were nearly 150 violet holdings on which a total of almost one million plants were grown mainly in glasshouses (for instance, in the 1920s Nelson Coon's Rhinebeck Floral Company had 19 glasshouses), although a small proportion were grown in frames. 'Marie Louise' was easily the most important cultivar, but some 'Lady Hume Campbell' (often referred to as 'Campbell'), 'Swanley White' and 'Farquhar' were also grown. These plants yielded about 60 million flowers annually, which were sold through the markets in New York City, Philadelphia, Buffalo and Chicago, as well as direct to florists in these cities, and in Cleveland, Pittsburgh and other large towns and cities.

Intensive cultivation under glass led to pest and disease attacks on 'Marie Louise', probably due to inadequate rotation and inefficient soil sterilization. 'Lady Hume Campbell', with its excellent constitution, was tried with success by many growers; indeed in 1903 at Torresdale, Philadelphia, R. M. Eisenhardt erected sufficient glass to house nearly 7,000 plants of this cultivar. Other growers were changing back to 'Neapolitan' and were also trying 'Duchesse de Parme', but the paler colours of all three were less sought-after at the markets, and more heat was required than was necessary for 'Marie Louise', and thus the growers' returns were lower and their expenses heavier. Allegedly disease-resistant sports of 'Marie Louise' were introduced, for example 'Farquhar' which was found growing healthily among diseased plants of 'Marie Louise' on Farquhars nursery at Roslindale, Massachusetts, and was first exhibited by a Mr McKay in the state capital, Boston, in January 1896. This cultivar was claimed to be larger, deeper in colour, longer-stemmed, more vigorous and freer-flowering than its parent. It was also earlier-flowering and finished earlier, but by planting 'Lady Hume Campbell' as well, a dearth of violet blossom late in the season could be avoided. It was reported in *The Garden and Forest* that the very highest claims were being made for 'Farquhar' and that it would entirely supersede 'Marie Louise'. However, T. D. Hatfield of Wellesley, Massachusetts, writing in the same periodical a few years later, stated that 'in some places it is as badly diseased as its parent and although we hoped so much from it we have had to fall back on the more reliable "Lady Hume Campbell" '. The resistance 'Lady Hume Campbell' showed to what had been thought overwhelming difficulties must have appeared almost miraculous to growers facing ruin; in 1920, after several more years of near disaster for growers of 'Marie Louise', Mr Taft, in *Greenhouse Management: A Manual for Florists and Flower Lovers* (Orange Judd, New York, 1920), was able to report that 'Lady Hume Campbell' was still quite free from disease. The importance that the violet enjoyed as a commercial horticultural crop led to the Department of Agriculture carrying out research into the troubles affecting the Parma violets. Eventually these were sufficiently successful to enable growers to continue cultivating both 'Marie Louise' and 'Farquhar'. As far as can be ascertained, the latter cultivar has never been grown in Britain under that name, but it could perhaps have been the sort offered for sale as 'Improved Marie Louise' by The Violet Nurseries, Henfield, England, and other nurseries early in the twentieth century.

'Mrs John J. Astor' probably originated in the USA and was described as darker and more vigorous than 'Madame Millet'; its remarkable rosy-heliotrope colour, exceptionally free-flowering habit and penetrating perfume led to its introduction in the UK in 1898 and it received the Royal Horticultural Society's Award of Merit when shown by the Hood Gardens of Totnes, Devon, on 7 November in the following year. It quickly became one of the most widely grown Parma cultivars, in spite of doubts that were being expressed regarding its weak stems and lack of hardiness (even by Parma standards).

Parma violets were being grown on a very large scale in the south of France for use in the manufacture of perfume, as well as for bunching, the chief centres being around Grasse, Vence and Cagnes. Large numbers of bunches were sent to various towns and cities in France as well as abroad. The numbers of bunches sent to London alone must have been considerable: in 1897 the *Journal of Horticulture* reported 'thousands of city clerks appear at the office every morning with a fresh bunch of violets in their buttonholes'; and until well after World War I, most of the violets handled by the London markets were from France although, in addition to those home produced, some also came from Italy. So popular were Parma violets that the *Gardeners Chronicle* recorded in October 1901 that *Achillea ptarmica flore pleno* was being dyed with aniline to resemble them, and then sold in London.

'Colcronan Hybrid' (commented on earlier in this chapter with reference to the alleged sterility of these violets) was listed in the UK from about 1901 onwards and was generally regarded as the largest-flowered Parma; its colour was similar to that of 'Lady Hume Campbell', but it came into flower earlier. Together with 'Parme de Toulouse', another cultivar resembling 'Lady Hume Campbell', it was valued for the Christmas market as a cut flower at the Violet Farm, Corfe Mullen.

Probably one of the hardiest Parma cultivars, 'Mrs Arthur' was first offered for sale in about 1902. It was very highly esteemed: William Artindale and Son of Ranmoor, Sheffield, England, described it as 'probably the best and most useful double violet yet raised', and some years later Mrs Grace L. Zambra of the Windward Violet Nurseries wrote 'our experience of it is very satisfactory, it is a wonderful grower, very free-flowering, so easy to propagate and a really happy doer'. Its flowers were of a fairly deep blue and were sometimes considered unattractive, but its ability to thrive where others had failed and to bring the unique Parma violet perfume into gardens were quite sufficient factors to ensure success. No record has been traced of this cultivar ever having been tried in the USA, where it might have proved resistant to at least some of the problems that beset the Parma cultivars there and would also have been deeper in colour than most of the substitutes that were being tried in place of 'Marie Louise'.

During the early years of the nineteenth century, increasing numbers of homes had electric lighting installed in place of gas or oil. Certain cultivars such as 'Madame Millet' and 'Mrs John J. Astor' looked attractive under all three forms of lighting but electricity made the hitherto-popular darker-coloured Parmas appear almost black, and so the demand for the paler sorts increased; only darker sorts, such as 'Marie Louise' with its outstanding perfume and 'Mrs Arthur', favoured because of its hardiness, were unaffected by this trend. New paler-coloured forms became popular: 'Mrs d'Arcy' was introduced in about 1902 and some years later 'Jamie Higgins', both of which were described as having silvery-mauve flowers. The former was very free-flowering and the latter, found as a sport in Jamison Higgins's garden at Bryanstone, near Blandford, England, was considered to be one of the hardiest Parmas and was introduced by Mr Kettle's Violet Farm at Corfe Mullen. Another violet of similar coloration was found at that establishment as a sport of 'Marie Louise' in 1912; this was named 'Mrs J. J. Kettle' and differed from the preceding cultivars in that the silvery-mauve colour was splashed with red, thus possibly indicating that it was derived from 'New York' rather than the true 'Marie Louise'. Its unique colouring and a very sweet perfume ensured that it became quite widely grown even at a time when the Parma violets were beginning to go out of fashion. This cultivar and 'Jamie Higgins' were imported by the Rhinebeck Floral Company, USA in the 1920s, thus possibly indicating a trend in favour of the paler sorts there too, but it was soon discovered that these also needed greater artificial winter heat than did 'Marie Louise'.

From about World War I onwards, interest in the Parma violets began to wane and few new cultivars were introduced. The most outstanding of the later introductions was 'Président Poincaré', a Millet introduction named after the French statesman who was president from 1913 to 1920; this cultivar had a powerful perfume, and the navy-blue colour of the flowers was quite distinct among Parma violets. The reason for the decline in interest in the single and hardy double violets is puzzling, but in the case of the Parma cultivars, possible explanations are easier to find. The single violets had been considerably improved by way of larger flowers and longer stems (see Chapter 2) and needed less attention than the Parmas required. The break-up of many large estates where they had been grown in quantity, and a severe reduction in the number of horticultural staff on many that survived, also contributed to the decline; in addition the lack of time, space and labour during the World Wars made it difficult for the more tender plants such as Parma violets to survive unaided. Many of the large general nurseries ceased growing these, and often other violets too, for economic reasons.

The profitable violet farms of southern England and the West Country were able to continue growing less profitable cultivars, as these could be subsidized by the cut-flower sales. Nevertheless, the reduction in demand for violet plants, which continued until the late 1960s, inevitably resulted in the disappearance of many cultivars, and again the Parmas were especially badly affected by this trend. By 1963 only four cultivars, 'Duchesse de Parme', 'Marie Louise', 'Mrs John J. Astor' and 'Swanley White', remained easily obtainable. Six years later only the first-named was still listed and 'Mrs John J. Astor' may have become extinct. Now, happily, with the revival of interest in violets of all kinds, 'Marie Louise' is again being offered for sale in addition to 'Duchesse de Parme'; 'Swanley White' and 'New York' are still being grown on a very small scale in England. In the USA 'Duchesse de Parme', 'Marie Louise' and 'Swanley White' were still being offered for sale in 1973.

SINGLE-FLOWERED PARMA VIOLETS

It would be wrong to end this account without making a brief reference to single-flowered Parmas, having only mentioned doubles above. It might be expected, as with many other plants having double flowers, that these have been derived from a single-flowered form, but very few references have been made to this. In 1883, a single-flowered cultivar with pale lavender flowers and a very sweet perfume was listed as *Viola odorata suavis pallida* or *italica*. It was alleged to produce double Parma sports and these in turn would sometimes revert. If this was correct, it must indicate that a single Parma was being grown, but nothing further has been traced about it and, in spite of the very widespread cultivation of the double Parmas, no reports have been discovered of singling of the flowers.

Then in 1895, Ermanno Bredemeier of Pallanza in north-west Italy introduced 'Principessa di Summunte', a single violet described as having exceptionally sweetly scented, perfectly formed flowers. Descriptions of the colour of the flowers vary from pale pink with darker edges, white ground heavily flaked with pale blue, white with veins of pale blue, to white with a picotee edge of clear blue. A writer in *Gardeners Chronicle* commented that it was the daintiest violet, almost a fairy-like little thing. The flowers were described as opening in large numbers at the same time on individual plants and it forced well. In 1906 it was reported as having appeared as a seedling in a garden at Roubaix, La Croix-Verte, near Saumur, Maine-et-Loire, France, and in time seedlings were produced there that bred true to the parent. The foliage of 'Principessa di Summunte' resembled that of the Parmas and its habit of flowering, its perfume and its colour all suggest that it was in fact a single-flowered Parma violet. It received the First Class Certificate of the French National Horticultural Society when exhibited by Millet in Paris in 1899; in Britain, J. C. House, of Isaac House and Son of Westbury-on-Trym, thought that it would have a great future, but unfortunately most growers only considered it as a curiosity, and despite its unique colour it may now be extinct.

Parma violets do not have to be cultivated following the old, time-consuming procedures, and in many places cloche protection will suffice; they should then amply reward anyone who acquires them, providing unique fragrance and beauty for garden and home in the bleak days of winter. Seedsmen are continually producing improved strains of seed and, in some cases, such as with some zonal pelargoniums, the grower raising plants by traditional means is being faced with increasing competition; however, as Parma violets rarely if ever set seed, the demand for plants will be unaffected. I believe that the business of selling these violets as pot plants in flower is due for a considerable revival – and the long-lasting flowers are so rarely seen in florists' shops that it would take a vast increase in production to saturate the market.

Since 1980, Parma violets have been observed in France with single flowers and also setting seed. The number of cultivars offered for sale has increased but the choice of colour is still regrettably restricted as neither 'Madame Millet' nor 'Mrs John J. Astor' appear to be in cultivation. This is particularly disappointing in the case of the latter as it was still obtainable in the early 1960s. The only other Parma violets listed by nurseries in the UK at that time were 'Comte di Brazza' ('Comte de Brazza' or 'Swanley White'), 'Duchesse de Parme' and 'New York' (then listed as 'Marie Louise'). Other Parma violets now offered for sale include 'd'Udine', 'Gloire de Verdun', 'Lady Hume Campbell', and 'Neapolitan'. New on the scene is the superb 'Ash Vale Blue' of only partly known origins. I suggest anyone obtaining Parma violets for the first time should include 'Duchesse de Parme' as this cultivar is usually the easiest to grow.

CULTIVARS OF SCENTED PARMA VIOLETS (TENDER)

'Ash Vale Blue'. Found by Mike Hardman on sale in Essex, England. The petals are mainly white with pale blue markings towards the edges. Distinct from the other Parma violets being offered for sale and possibly a rediscovery of a 'lost' cultivar.

'Cannell's Blue and White' (Cannell, 1880). Porcelain blue and white.

'Carter's Mazarine Blue' (Carter, 1890). No description available.

'Clarence Castle' (1897). Mauvish-pink.

'Colcronan Hybrid' (1901). Lavender-blue, was often regarded as the largest Parma cultivar.

'**Conte di Brazza**' (Conte di Brazza, Italy, 1880). FCC, RHS, 1883. White with slight pale blue tints. Also listed as 'Swanley White' and 'White Parma'. Still in cultivation in Britain and the USA. MRCF.

'**Countess of Caledon**'. No description has been traced but 'admirably grown' plants were shown at a RHS meeting on 8 March 1904 and, subsequently, by the Hon. Mrs Albert Brassey, Heythrop Park, Chipping Norton, Oxfordshire.

'**Dowager Lady Williams Wynn**' (Wynn, 1900; sport of 'Conte di Brazza'). Pale blue.

'**Duchesse de Parme**' (1870). Lavender-blue 88D-86D. Probably the easiest to grow of the Parma cultivars. MRCF.

'**Duchess of Edinburgh**' (1877). White petals edged with pale blue. Sometimes tinted with mauve. Exhibited by R. W. Beachey at the Torquay Chrysanthemum Show in November 1894.

'**d'Udine**' (Italy 1903). Some stocks have slight reddish streaks and are similar to some stocks offered as 'Marie Louise'; however, this cultivar is nearer to a blue 88B. Possibly only listed in France 20 years ago, it is now quite widely available.

'**Evelyn Kelly**' (Newton Abbot, Devon, 1930). Dark blue. Resembled 'Marie Louise' but, according to Mrs Grace L. Zambra, much easier to grow.

'**Farquhar**' (Farquhar, USA, 1896; 'Marie Louise' sport). Slightly deeper-coloured flowers than parent. Selected for its disease resistance, also allegedly larger, more floriferous and with longer stems. The flowering season was also claimed to be earlier than its parent, both in terms of starting and finishing flowering.

'**Fee Jalucine**' (Nathalie Casbas, Villaudric, France, 1999). Despite confident statements that Parma violets do not produce seed, it has been known for a considerable time that they do. This is a selection from 'Parme de Toulouse' seed.

'**Feline**' (Casbas, France; from 'Parme de Toulouse'). Single-flowered lavender-pink.

'**Gloire d'Angoulême**', see 'Lady Hume Campbell'.

'**Gloire de Verdun**'. The first references to this name are from the 1970s in France. Smaller mauve 85A flowers on shorter stems. Plants are somewhat more compact, offering possibilities as a flowering pot plant.

'**Hopley's White**'. At first glance this violet obtained from New Zealand appears to be a white Parma. It has the tendency to exhibit green tints rather than the blue tints sometimes seen with 'Conte di Brazza' and the flowers have been described as being of better form than that cultivar. My opinion of 'Conte di Brazza' is that when grown well the flowers are of good form. It is usually stated that Parma violets have a unique perfume and I believe that 'Hopley's White' has that same perfume. The possibility may be present that this is a rare hybrid, having a Parma violet for one of its parents.

'**Imperial**' (USA; 'Marie Louise' sport). Similar to 'Farquhar'.

'**Jamie Higgins**' (Kettle, 1913). Pale lavender. J. J. Kettle recorded the Dorset origins of this cultivar (see earlier in this chapter). There is a view that the cultivar originated in the USA but at present I prefer Kettle's account in which he did not claim to have raised it, though he has wrongly been credited with having done so. Mrs Grace L. Zambra considered this the hardiest Parma cultivar and mentioned that the pale colour in some soils could be overcome with an occasional dosing with liquid soot or manure. Also listed as 'Mrs Higgins'.

'John Roberts' ('Marie Louise' sport). Paler in colour than parent. Exhibited at RHS meeting on 16 March 1901.

'La Belle Paris' or **'La Belle Parisienne'** (1913). Lavender. Long stems. Regarded by some growers, but by no means all, as identical to 'Duchesse de Parme'. Listed in 1930s.

'Lady Cowper' (1913). No description available. Exhibited by R. Staward of Hertford at a RHS meeting on 18 March 1913.

'Lady Elsington' (Northumberland; 'Conte di Brazza' sport, 1877). Pale blue.

'Lady Hume Campbell' (1875). Imported by Lady Hume Campbell from Milan some years before its introduction. A superb lavender-mauve 90D cultivar. Valued for flowering late, so prolonging the season, and for its disease resistance. Listed in the 1950s. Mrs Grace L. Zambra stated that 'Gloire d'Angoulême' and 'Parme de Toulouse' were identical to 'Lady Hume Campbell'. Other growers, including J. J. Kettle, considered 'Parme de Toulouse' to be earlier flowering. If 'Gloire d'Angoulême' and 'Lady Hume Campbell' were identical, bearing in mind the circumstances surrounding its introduction, the former could in fact be the correct name. The plants I supplied originated from Nelson Coon, Massachusetts, USA. The plants thus came back to Devon in the 1970s, having been exported by the Devon grower, R. W. Beachey, to Massachusetts in 1892. MRCF.

'Lady Waldie Griffith' (1913). White flowers.

'Madame Millet' (Néant, France, 1868, but not introduced until 1884). Lilac-rose. Described at that time as an exact match for the fashion shade of heliotrope. The cultivar was introduced, but not raised, by Millet despite at least one claim to the contrary. Although formerly quite widely listed, it is no longer obtainable. Exhibited by R. W. Beachey at the November 1894 Torquay Chrysanthemum Show. MRCF.

'Madame Pethers' (Pethers, 1905). Blue flowers.

'Marie Louise' (Schuer, Baden, 1865; but believed to be older). Deep lavender-mauve. Very fragrant flowers capable of reaching large proportions. At Stocksfield-on-Tyne, Northumberland, flowers 3 cm (1 1/4 in) across on stems in excess of 17 cm (7 in) were recorded. For many years the most widely grown cultivated violet in the USA. Some stocks have reddish streaks but the earliest descriptions made no mention of these and later accounts stated the red-streaked form to be 'New York'. One French nursery in the 1970s made no mention of red streaks on 'Marie Louise' but did refer to 'd'Udine' having such streaks. An article of mine concerning this matter was published in *The Plantsman* (see Bibliography). MRCF.

'Mrs Arthur' (1902). Deep bluish-lavender. One of the hardiest Parma cultivars. MRCF.

'Mrs d'Arcy' (1902). Silvery-mauve.

'Mrs Higgins', see 'Jamie Higgins'.

'Mrs John J. Astor' (USA, 1895). AM, RHS,1899. Rosy-lavender. Listed in the early 1960s. A 'lost' violet cultivar, still not rediscovered. Described by F. W. Burbidge as having a 'decided heliotrope perfume'.

'Mrs J. J. Kettle' (Kettle, 1912; described as a sport of 'Marie Louise' but possibly really of 'New York'). Silvery-mauve splashed with red. J. C. House described it as having an extremely delicate colour and a delightful fragrance. Listed in the 1940s.

'Miss Mantoni' (1892). Bright violet-blue. Free flowering, compact habit.

'Neapolitan', see 'Pallida plena'.

'New York' (1869). Deep lavender-mauve 86C with red markings. Also listed as *Viola odorata pendula* (the 'Weeping Violet of New York'). Still grown in Britain and the USA.

'Pallida plena'. Presumably the original form found in Asia. Pale lavender 89C. Listed in the 1930s and, after an interval, available again. Also listed as 'Neapolitan'.

'Parmaensis Flore Pleno' (1863). White striped rose flowers.

'Parme de Toulouse'. Mauve 88C with paler centre. The cultivar associated with the revival of violet growing at Toulouse. Distinct from 'Lady Hume Campbell'.

'Parme Sans Filets'. A form of this class of violet that did not produce runners.

'Perfection' (1885). Pale blue, but deeper and also earlier than 'Duchesse de Parme'. Attracted attention when exhibited by Isaac House and Son at the Bristol Chrysanthemum Show in 1903. Listed in the 1930s. Also listed as 'Perfecta'.

'Président Poincaré' (Millet, France, 1925). Navy blue. Powerful perfume.

'Principessa di Summunte'. Possibly a single-flowered Parma cultivar.

'Principessa Marguerite di Savoie' (1881). Deep mauvish-lavender (see page 72 and 73).

'Queen Mary' (1915). Usually described as deep violet-blue, but occasionally as pale mauve.

'Reine Louise' (1873). No description available.

'Robert Garret' (Cook, USA, 1888; 'Conte di Brazza' sport). Pale blue, exceptionally large blooms up to 3.75 cm (1 1/2 in) across.

'Ruhm von Cassell' (1890). No description available.

'Venice' (1880). Deep lavender-blue.

'White Marie Louise' (1896). Thought to be a white sport of 'Marie Louise'.

NOTES

1. Alphonse Karr, *A Tour Round My Garden* (Routledge, 1855).
2. Gabriel Tergit, *Flowers Through the Ages* (Wolff, 1961).

6

SOME VIOLA SPECIES

(MOSTLY HARDY)

In addition to *Viola odorata* and *V. suavis*, several other single-flowered viola species, and cultivated forms thereof, can be used to provide garden decoration and, in some cases, cut flowers, too. Bedding and exhibition violas and show and fancy pansies, violettas – which resemble small-flowered bedding violas (tufted pansies), as well as the cultivated forms of *V. gracilis* and *V. cornuta*, are beyond the scope of this guide. However, in passing, it is noted that cultivars of the last-mentioned species have been grown commercially to provide bunches of 'violets', notably 'Jersey Gem', raised by T. A. Weston of New Jersey, USA, 'Purpurea' and 'Papillio' as revealed in the 29 April 1907 issue of the *Journal of Horticulture and Home Farmer*:

> 'The street flower-sellers of London have discovered that *Viola* "Papillio" furnishes an excellent large flowered 'Violet', which, of course, it resembles both in colour and form. After all 'fair exchange is no robbery'.'

However, the writer failed to mention that the substitute flowers lacked the sweet perfume for which the scented violet is so highly regarded.

Many of the viola species will provide a fine display, and their often large, though usually unscented, flowers will extend the flowering season until the first flowers appear on the scented violets. A large number of these species come from North America and so much a part of the wild flora are these plants that they have been adopted as the emblems for the Canadian province of New Brunswick, and Illinois, New Jersey, Rhode Island and Wisconsin in the USA.

Cultivation of these violas should be carried out in a similar fashion to the scented violets. Apart from *Viola hederacea*, *V. labradorica* and *V. sulfurea*, runners are not usually produced, so propagation by division should be resorted to; however, many grow readily from seed. The three species mentioned above, together with *V. alpina* and *V. arenaria*, do not lose their leaves in winter; the remainder have a rootstock somewhat resembling a rhizome on the surface of the soil. However, when the leaves have died down, these can easily be missed, so the position of the clumps should be carefully marked so as to prevent disturbance when weeding in winter and early spring. The most spectacular of the species are the American Giant Violets. There is a

Viola declinata, V. pedafida, V. labradorica (riviniana), V. fujisun, V. hederacea,
V. sieboldiana, and *V. odorata* (drawing by Yvonne Matthews).

difference of opinion among botanists as to the nomenclature of these plants and this is reflected by confusion in the nursery lists. Considerable credit is due to other writers who have attempted to bring order to this situation; however, I am taking the easy way out, firstly by only mentioning those I have grown and secondly by largely avoiding naming the violets concerned, as it would be impossible for me to come up with the correct naming when botanists working in the field cannot do so as yet.

Type 1. Purchased as *V. cucullata*, the flowers are true violet in colour, not violet-blue shading to indigo (Mrs Grace L. Zambra's description of *V. c. grandiflora*). The flowers are fine for picking and come as the 'Governor Herrick' type violets are finishing.

Type 2. Obtained as *V. sororia*. Similar to the above, but with white flowers having a large royal blue centre. This seems certainly to be *V. priceana* (the Confederate Violet) but not only are there doubts about which species it is a form of, but also about its name. *The New York Times Magazine* of 21 March 1926 contained an article by Henry J. Brockmeyer in which the name was given as princeana after its principal grower at Bowling Green, Kentucky. Plants obtained in the 1970s as *V. septemtrionalis alba* have proved to be of this type, but *V. septemtrionalis* plants from another source have been of *Type 5* below. This is a spectacular flower and, like the others, excellent for cut-flower purposes.

Type 3. Again similar in flower form and foliage to both the above. Obtained as *V. septemtrionalis rubra*, it has very attractive rosy purple 77A flowers. Possibly it may be that listed by Roy Genders as *V. cucullata rubra* (rich purple-red) but the mottling of the foliage mentioned by that writer[1] is absent from any of these violets that I have grown, the foliage of which at a glance resembles violets of the type of 'Governor Herrick', but the latter do not lose their leaves in winter. 'Red Giant' is similar in flower but there could be differences as to length of flowering season and appearance of foliage. These should be compared growing in the same conditions.

Type 4. Palest lilac or white flowers minutely dotted with violet. Listed as *V. cucullata thurstoni* or *V. c.* 'Freckles', there remains a doubt as to whether it really is a form of that species. Until reassured by the experts, I will remain dubious about plants with flowers of this type, as the colour breaking may be due to the presence of a virus.

Type 5. Stocks obtained as *V. cucullata albiflora*, *V. striata*, *V. septrionalis* and *V.* 'White Ladies' all seem identical. The flowers are white with a greenish centre and slight, almost black rays. The petals are rounded, so giving the flower a more substantial, circular appearance. The leaves are darker green than the above-listed types, wider for their length and shorter than the flower stalks. A most desirable plant.

All the above set seed and hybridization can occur, which does not help the botanists especially when the plants are also distributed widely in the wild. 'Pink Gem', described as a form of V. *cucullata*, was found by Joseph Meehan in about 1901, growing wild in Massachusetts. It was described as the first clear-pink hardy violet. Although 'Pink Gem' may no longer be in cultivation, other forms are: for example the Lamb Nurseries of Spokane, Washington listed 'Alice Witter' (white with red centre), 'Red Giant' and 'Snow Princess' in 1977. Violets of this type, probably crossed with V. *odorata* and V. *hirta*, quite likely gave 'Governor Herrick' and similar cultivars which are mentioned in Chapter 2.

There is less controversy as to the naming of the remaining species, which are listed in alphabetical order:

adunca. An American species with foliage almost intermediate between the violets and V. *cornuta*. Pretty rose flowers.

alpina. A free-flowering species with small carmine flowers.

arenaria. Another free-flowering species. The flowers are pale lilac and produced in summer. *Rosea* is a bright rose form. Also listed as V. *reichenbachiana* and V. *rupestris*.

'Delmonden'. Certificate of Preliminary Commendation, Joint Rock-Garden Plant Committee of the RHS, the Alpine Garden Society and the Scottish Rock Garden Club, 1967. Of quite recent introduction, this is believed to be a naturally occurring hybrid between *Viola pedatifida* and V. *septemtrionalis*. It has large blue 94C flowers and the divided foliage resembles V. *pedatifida*. This most attractive violet was found in the garden of Miss A. Foster, Delmonden, Hawkhurst, Kent, England.

hederacea. Creeping habit. White flowers with bluish-purple 80B centres. Probably not a viola but rather a similar plant which evolved in Australasia, hence its alternative name, *Erpetion reniforme*. This species, while not fully hardy in Britain, will make an excellent plant for the cool greenhouse. A selection from this with blue 94C flowers is named 'Baby Blue'.

jooi. This species, with large creamy-mauve 75A flowers, received the AM, RHS in 1974. V. *macroceras* from Asia is similar.

labradorica. From Newfoundland, Canada, and the USA. Rather similar to V. *canina*, except that the foliage is dull purple. The flowers are lilac 86C. Sometimes listed as V. *l. purpurea*.

macroceras, see *Jooi*.

reichenbachiana, *rupestris*, see *Arenaria*.

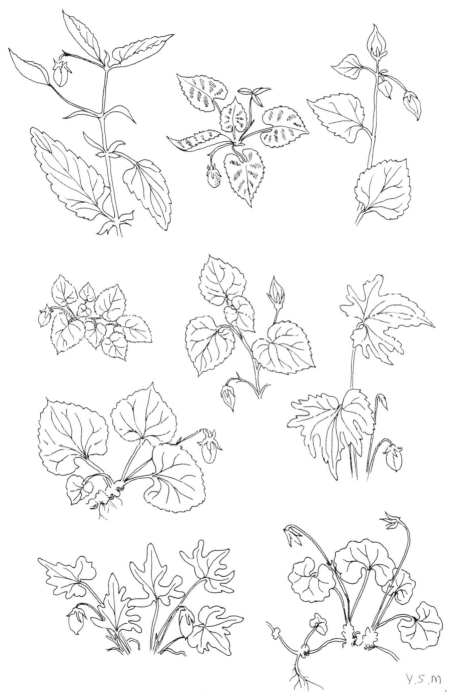

Y.S.M

Viola species, top row: *V. elatior, V. selkirkii, V. pennsylvanica (pubescens* var *eriocarpa*); second row: *V. patrinii* (with *V. sororaria* below), *V. labradorica, V. dissecta*; bottom row: *V. pedatifida, V. pedata.*

sulfurea or **vilmorini**. Probably a native of south-central France and similar to, but distinct from, *V. odorata*. One of the major differences is a lack of scent although it has been referred to as the yellow sweet violet. The correct specific name has been in doubt for many years, as the plant appeared from more than one source at about the same time; it must, however, be *Sulfurea* or *Vilmorini*. The following names are not correct but have been used: 'Sulphurea' (a bedding viola which received the RHS Award of Merit in 1913), *glabella* (which is in fact a different species with yellow flowers on branching stems), 'Yellow Queen', 'Yellowette', 'Yellowrette', 'Pallida' (also used for single Parma violets), *aurantiaca* and *lutea*. It is stressed that the Royal Horticultural Society's Award of Merit was bestowed on the bedding viola 'Sulphurea' and not on this species, as is sometimes stated, as for instance in the 1964 catalogue issued by Hillier and Sons of Winchester. *V. sulfurea* was introduced by Leon Chenault of Orleans, France, having been found near Forez and Lyons. It was exhibited at an RHS meeting by Robert Veitch and Son of Exeter, Devon on 17 April 1897. Vilmorin-Andrieux listed this violet as *V. vilmorini*. There was a controversy in France as to whether this should be listed as a form of *V. odorata* or as a separate species; in my opinion the lack of scent and unique colour are quite sufficient reasons, although admittedly non-botanical, for giving it specific rank. An additional complication is that while the original growers of this violet in France considered it scentless, some growers including Roy Genders have referred to the 'pleasing woodland fragrance of the blooms'.[2] Early in the twentieth century some nurseries were referring to *sulfurea* as the khaki-coloured violet, a description which does not seem to fit the pretty creamy-primrose 8C flowers with deep apricot centres. However, Roy Genders referred to a form with creamy-buff flowers called 'Irish Elegance' and this was illustrated in *Alpines in Colour and Cultivation*.[3] Although considerably paler than khaki, these descriptions could perhaps refer to the same violet. It may well be that 'Irish Elegance' was scented, hence the cause of this confusion, too.

NOTES

1. Roy Genders, *Pansies, Violas and Violets* (John Gifford, 1958).
2. Roy Genders, *Collecting Hardy Plants for Interest and Profit* (Stanley Paul, 1959).
3. T. C. Mansfield, *Alpines in Colour and Cultivation* (Britain in Pictures, 1952).

7
VIOLET HYBRIDIZERS

Over the years most new violet cultivars have been discovered in the wild or in gardens as chance seedlings. Violet seed is rarely produced by the really large-flowered cultivars; indeed it seems that the larger and more stately the flower, the smaller the number of fertile seeds that will be obtained. The seedlings are nearly always identical to the parent plant as they are mostly produced from the closed or cleistogamic flowers which are self-pollinating.

The raising of seedlings with the object of obtaining improved cultivars has no guarantee of success – 'a patient, persevering and unrewarded race' is how E. J. Perfect aptly termed the violet raisers.[1] Seeds of many cultivars were saved at the Windward Violet Nurseries and at The Violet Farm, Corfe Mullen, England. Mrs Grace L. Zambra of the former establishment described it as 'one of our most interesting experiments, the raising of seeds, if not a very profitable one',[2] and only a few worthwhile results were obtained.

Yet a very few people, either as a result of long experience or innate brilliance, were able to induce the violet to produce seedlings out of all proportion to the cultivars they were working with. Edward A. Bunyard wrote that violets had not slowly increased in size, but instead a giant – 'The Czar' – suddenly appeared and the offspring were of this size.[3] However, this statement is hard to accept. Without any doubt, 'The Czar' played a considerable part in the breeding of other cultivars, and most of the more recent cultivars have 'The Czar' in their ancestry, whilethe progeny of its contemporary cultivars, such as 'Devoniensis' and 'The Giant', have not stayed the course. 'The Czar', though, was not a great deal larger than other violets at the time it was introduced and there is no doubt that later introductions, such as the range of Millet seedlings from 'Gloire de Bourg-la-Reine' to 'Souvenir de Ma Fille', are much larger. One could perhaps say that two giants appeared suddenly, which influenced later sorts, firstly 'The Czar' and secondly, 20 or so years later, 'Gloire de Bourg-la-Reine'. Certainly the latter completely changed the market; at the time that 'Princesse de Galles', one of its offspring, reached Britain, J. J. Kettle was in the process of building up stocks of a promising seedling, but he wrote that it was immediately put in the shade by the new violet. Likewise a great future was predicted for 'Wellsiana'; writers in *Gardeners Chronicle* in 1887 stated that one day it would become the most widely grown cut-flower cultivar, as it had twice as many flowers as 'The Czar', was more fragrant, was larger and deeper and was easier to grow. As late as 1891, *The Garden* was describing 'Wellsiana' as the giant among the singles, but within the next year or so statements like this would have become utterly obsolete with the arrival of 'Princesse de Galles' and other Millet seedlings. Nevertheless, it seems more likely that the violet has steadily developed in size over the years, with apparent sudden increases in size coinciding with periods when able hybridizers were at work.

Information about the violet raisers has been difficult to acquire and the following accounts are not as detailed as one would wish. Armand Millet, the most famous of the raisers, has been dealt with at some length, as has George Lee whose creations were the result of honest endeavour coupled with an ability to advertise his seedlings to the best advantage. The cultivars raised by J. J. Kettle were the most sensational of all and although the following account at first glance appears much too short to be at all comprehensive, it should be remembered that most of Kettle's important seedlings were semi-doubles; see Chapter 4 in which they are dealt with at some length. G. W. Boothby deserves mention but the remaining raisers until recent years have given us, at the most, two important cultivars each and these are dealt with in the general text and lists of cultivars.

G. W. BOOTHBY

From the English town of Louth, Lincolnshire, G. W. Boothby was one of the earliest of the violet raisers and he also contributed to horticultural periodicals. There is some evidence that he used particularly the then popular cultivar 'The Giant' as a seed parent. Cultivars that he raised included 'Beauty of Louth' (c.1870), 'Giantess', one of the few white cultivars (1873) and 'Floribunda', bluish-purple (1880). Some of Boothby's seedlings were tried out by George Lee, but none became widely grown.

JOHN J. KETTLE

Founder of The Violet Farm, Corfe Mullen in 1905 (see Chapter 8), John J. Kettle is also mainly remembered for his semi-double violets such as 'Countess of Shaftesbury' (see Chapter 4). Other cultivars raised by him included 'Corfe Mullen Wonder', 'Lobelia' and 'Steel Blue', but I have failed to trace any descriptions of these. The Parma violet, 'Mrs J. J. Kettle' occurred as a sport at The Violet Farm. The later years of his life, when the advanced seedlings were being raised, are less well documented than those preceding. He did write the section on violets for two books published by the *Daily Express* and numerous notes on the cultivation of violets and other crops, but little of this interesting material has been published (see Bibliography).

Two of his seedlings received awards of merit from the Royal Horticultural Society: 'Mrs David Lloyd George' (1918) and 'Princess Mary' (1924), in 1925 and 1928 respectively; they were also awarded gold medals at the New York Flower Show, as well as other medals and ribbons in the USA, after being imported there by the Rhinebeck Floral Company of New York State. It seems more than a little surprising that no important awards have ever been made to 'Countess of Shaftesbury' as the flowers were more beautiful and the plants just as reliable as those of its predecessors.

An article of mine about J. J. Kettle and his Violet Farm was published in the *Journal of the Royal Horticultural Society* (see Bibliography).

GEORGE LEE

George Lee was a market gardener at Clevedon, Somerset, an English seaside resort on the Bristol Channel coast. Over the years Mr Lee increasingly specialized in violets which he grew for cutting. The flowers of a seedling that appeared there, which was regarded as a cross between 'The Czar' and 'Devoniensis', readily found buyers. This cultivar was named 'Victoria Regina' and Lee raised seedlings from it. It did not take him long to realize that his violets would appeal to amateur gardeners as well as to cut-flower growers.

It is interesting to note that at about this time Armand Millet in France was crossing 'The Czar' with 'Wilson', and both 'Wilson' and 'Devoniensis' were often regarded as forms of *Viola suavis*, so both hybridizers were working simultaneously along very similar lines. Lee sent flowers and foliage of 'Victoria Regina' to the editor of *The Florist and Pomologist* in March 1873, and an item appeared describing this cultivar as being extremely large flowered with evenly expanded petals, and the colour as deep violet-purple. Frost damage had affected them but the previous year the flowers had measured as much as 3 cm (1¼ in) across. Lee had described a batch of 30 seedlings he had raised from 'Victoria Regina' which had flowered and which he regarded as 'a new race of violets, no two being alike, not even in leaf, some were much rounder than others, several had white centres, so that we may eventually hope for some with margins like pansies and of several shades of colour too'. The editor wrote that 'Victoria Regina' was without doubt the finest of all large-flowered sweet violets which had yet been obtained. In December 1873 an article by Lee appeared in the same periodical; this included an outline of violet cultivation, a survey of cultivars in commerce and a review of his seedlings. He mentioned a new cultivar he had raised called 'Prince Consort' which he described as rather similar to 'The Czar' in growth and with flowers larger than those of 'Victoria Regina' but more inclined to fade.

In 1874 Lee showed 'Victoria Regina' at a meeting of the Royal Horticultural Society, but while it was thought to be an improvement on 'The Czar', having rounder and broader petals, it was not considered sufficiently different to warrant the award of a First Class Certificate. However, in July 1876 Richard Dean of Ealing, famous for his violas and primroses (Dean's hybrid coloured primroses remained obtainable from seedsmen for many years), wrote that he considered 'Victoria Regina' more robust and far superior to 'The Czar', which he had consequently discarded. Some years later it was stated in the catalogue of Henry Cannell's Swanley Nurseries that 'Victoria Regina' had to be regularly replanted; otherwise it would be scarcely distinct from 'The Czar' and 'The Giant'.

The editor of *The Florist and Pomologist* had no hesitation in recommending this cultivar: 'On several occasions during the blooming season we have seen flowers of Mr G. Lee's violet "Prince Consort" which is the finest variety yet raised as to form, and deep purple, [it] completely eclipses "The Czar" with which it has been compared.' The editor of *The Garden*, while obviously satisfied with the merits of Lee's violets in general, seemed less confident: 'Although better than "Victoria Regina", but not much, these two will soon be universally grown.'

Lee announced in 1876 that he required orders totalling £1,000 before he would be prepared to release plants of 'Prince Consort', thus allowing other nurseries to obtain stocks and so compete. However, he introduced another seedling in the orthodox way, this being 'Odoratissima' which was listed in the Cannell catalogue of 1877 as 'the best violet ever sent out, king of all singles although not quite so early as "Victoria Regina". It is at first sight like "Victoria Regina" but pansy shaped; in size and roundness it resembles a pansy'.

The *Gardeners Chronicle*, in acknowledging sample flowers sent by Henry Cannell, commented: 'The flowers were remarkably large and the scent exquisite – you may well say these have the appearance of a pansy in size and form and that this is the king of the tribe.' It was stated in the *Journal of Horticulture and Home Farmer*: ' "Odoratissima" is the grandest of all single purple violets.'

The Florist and Pomologist also joined in this extremely favourable reception:

'Mr Lee's new violet "Odoratissima" well deserves the name – and so far as can be judged from cut flowers – is the best of the recent novelties. Large finely formed broad rounded well-set petals [of a] bright shade of blue-purple. Delicious fragrance. The foliage is not so coarse as in some of the other large-flowered varieties. Wonderful powerful perfume. Effective and attractive colour.' The writer was obviously so enthusiastic that he failed to realize that he was virtually repeating earlier remarks. This cultivar was an immediate success and had a comparatively dwarf habit; it was also considered hardier than 'Victoria Regina'. R. W. Beachey wrote that it was the bluest violet in his extensive collection. Such was the frequency with which new cultivars were being taken up, that by 1889 'Odoratissima' was being superseded and in *Gardeners Chronicle* it was stated that it was then mainly being grown for its leaves to back bunches of flowers from other varieties.

Although 'Victoria Regina' had been considered by many to be superseded by 'Odoratissima', it was not without support. One grower wrote in October

1880: 'That very fine violet "Victoria Regina" is now blooming freely, it is decidedly the best single as much ahead of "The Czar" as "The Czar" was ahead of "Devoniensis".' For some while 'Victoria Regina' was the most sought-after violet at Covent Garden Market and one of the growers at Hounslow, who probably sent flowers to that market, wrote of Lee's cultivars: 'This superb violet ['Prince Consort'] raised by Lee of Clevedon bears remarkably fine blooms, the petals are broad and of great substance and the colour rich bluish violet. I have had this and "Victoria Regina" flowering for several weeks and quantities of fine plants lifted into six-inch [15-cm] pots promise to furnish supplies of bloom all the winter.'

According to J. C. House in the *Journal of the Royal Horticultural Society*, April 1917, Lee used to send a large bunch of 'Victoria Regina' violets to Queen Victoria at Balmoral over many years.

George Lee also worked actively with other seedlings; flowers of a white cultivar were favourably received by the horticultural press. In the autumn of 1879, he presented blooms of 'Argentiflora', described as being pale purple, but nearly white in winter and with an almost perpetual flowering season. Other descriptions of the colour were purplish-white and light blue mingled with white. In 1886, it was stated in an article in the *Journal of Horticulture and Home Farmer* that it originated from a cross between a purple cultivar and a white cultivar.

It seems that by 1880 'Prince Consort' had been released, even though it was stated in the *Journal of Horticulture and Home Farmer* in 1886 that it still had not been sent out. A violet named 'Prince Consort' 'raised' by Mr Underdown of Bovey Tracey, Devon, was mentioned in the issue of *The Garden* dated 17 April 1880 and this would seem to indicate that Lee had released some plants, unless another cultivar had been given the same name. Besides the Hounslow grower already mentioned, a gardener in Kent was claiming to have been supplied with it in 1881, but it did not appear in the catalogues of the leading nurseries.

'Princess of Prussia' was the last of Lee's seedlings of which a record has been traced. Again there were doubts as to when, or even if, it had been released. R. W. Beachey wrote in December 1881 that he had been growing it for more than a year and described it as the finest single sweet violet, much superior to 'Odoratissima' and 'Victoria Regina' and being of a rich purple colour and of the same size as 'Victoria Regina', but freer-flowering. However, a writer in the *Journal of Horticulture and Home Farmer* claimed that up to then it had not been introduced. By 1885 it was being offered for sale; Thomas S. Ware's catalogue described it as 'by far the grandest, even eclipsing the famous "Victoria Regina"'. In 1898 it was described as being similar to 'Wellsiana' and in the following year in the same periodical, it was called one of the better forms of 'The Czar'. G. Abbey, who at that time frequently wrote about violets, pointed out that although the flowers of 'Princess of Prussia' were as large as those of 'Victoria Regina', the latter produced twice as many flowers. He also provided the following statistics:

	'Prince Consort'	'Victoria Regina'	'Princess of Prussia'
Flower size	4.5 cm (1¾ in)	3.75 cm (1½ in)	3.75 cm (1½ in)
Stem length	23 cm (9 in)	18 cm (7 in)	15 cm (6 in)

George Lee's violets initially made a great impact and, together with 'Wellsiana' and 'The Czar', would have continued to be grown on a large scale for many years in the UK, had not the new French cultivars arrived in a wide range of colour and with even more shapely flowers. Abroad, George Lee's violets did not become widely grown, the cultivar grown in France as 'Reine Victoria' probably being distinct from 'Victoria Regina' (see following notes on Armand Millet). 'Victoria Regina' was, however, tried out in the USA but at that time Parma violets were becoming popular, and it was not surprising that it did not become established. In Germany 'Victoria Regina' met with at least limited success; a seedling raised by Zeiner of Bornstedt, Potsdam in about 1892, 'Frau Hof Gartendirektor Jühlke', was a cross between 'Victoria Regina' and 'Russian Superb' and in 1904 it was reported that 'Victoria Regina' was being successfully grown under glass in the Hamburg area.

ARMAND MILLET

Without doubt, Armand Millet must rate as the most successful of the comparatively small number of violet hybridizers. For more than 40 years a succession of cultivars were introduced from Millet's nursery at Bourg-la-Reine near Paris. These violets were of a remarkably high standard: both in numbers and in quality, Millet's seedlings were unusual in a plant that is notoriously difficult to hybridize and in which most of the advances have been from chance seedlings, both hitherto and in recent years.

Although Millet worked with a range of cultivars, it was by crossing 'The Czar' and 'Wilson' that the cultivars that made him so famous were evolved. The resulting seedlings had rounded petals and more circular flowers, rather like George Lee's 'Odoratissima' from a similar cross, but as the type evolved, another distinctive feature was evident: the large, rounded leaves. The flower shape is commonplace today, as typified by 'Princesse de Galles', which has been widely grown for scented cut-flower production in Britain. The fact that these violets can now be described as 'commonplace' is in itself a tribute to their raiser. In addition, Millet carried out further crosses among the smaller-flowered cultivars and seedlings of various colours were produced, some being quite novel.

One of the first of Armand Millet's new seedlings was 'Le Lilas' which was introduced in 1876, and described as very early, hardy and free-flowering. The colour, lilac heliotrope, although quite pretty, did not find favour when tried out as a market cut flower in France and it was rarely grown in Britain, although at the Henfield Violet Farm it was regarded as a good cultivar for growing in frames. In the previous year a seedling of 'Le Lilas' crossed with 'The Czar' was raised, named 'Brune de Bourg-la-Reine'; this coppery-purple cultivar was the first to have a metallic sheen, a characteristic later exemplified by 'Explorateur Dybowski' and 'La France'. Millet recommended this violet as a cut flower but it does not seem to have been widely grown, which was a pity as its colour was quite distinct. The cultivar named 'Millet' appeared in about 1876 and was the largest-flowered violet raised at Bourg-la-Reine up to that point and was probably the result of a cross between 'The Czar' and 'Wilson'. Millet claimed at one time that this violet was a predecessor of 'The Czar', but as the latter had reached France by 1868, it is unlikely. James Kelway and Sons of the Royal Nurseries, Langport, Somerset in England, one of the very few British nurseries to offer it for sale, described 'Millet' in 1898 as a single blue violet, with very large flowers and a sweet perfume; it remained in their catalogue until 1907. 'Millet' was also grown in Switzerland. It was renamed 'Souvenir de Millet Père' at an unknown date.

In 1878, one of the very few variegated-leaved violets, 'Armandine Millet' appeared in a bed of seedlings obtained from various crosses. Although initially described as having yellow or golden markings, later descriptions of the variegations mention them as being white or silver; for instance the Henfield Violet Farm recommended 'its elegant silver foliage' (see also page 51). In the following year 'Gloire de Bourg-la-Reine' was introduced, this being a logical development from 'Millet' in that the parentage was probably the same, but the flowers were larger. It was described as the giant of the family and the 'Paul Neyron' of violets (the Hybrid Perpetual rose 'Paul Neyron' still listed in catalogues was, and probably is, the largest in cultivation), and became a parent of other Millet introductions. Besides its size, the beautiful deep violet-blue colour, long stems, strong scent and fine dark foliage ensured its quite widespread cultivation in France and especially in Britain, where in 1890 R. W. Beachey stated that he was growing this 'very beautiful clear blue' violet at Kingskerswell, Devon.

Millet exhibited several violets at a meeting of the Central Horticultural Society of France on 17 April 1880. These included 'Brune de Bourg-la-Reine', 'Souvenir de Millet père', 'Armandine Millet', which was awarded the Society's First Class Certificate and 'Sans Pareille', similarly awarded, which was described as being of 'The Czar' type, with flower and foliage larger than any other cultivar then in existence. It was early flowering and had the rounded petals that were becoming so typical of the large-flowered Millet seedlings.

'Sans Pareille' did not become widely grown in this country, possibly due to the almost bewildering succession of new French violets that were being imported, preventing attention from being concentrated on any particular violet unless it was really outstanding; before long other violets with larger flowers were produced. However, R. W. Beachey wrote in the *Journal of Horticulture and Home Farmer* that he had obtained plants from Millet, and he regarded it as a very fine cultivar.

Edward A. Bunyard wrote in *The New Flora and Silva* that the cultivar 'Czar Bleu' (renamed in Provence, 'Reine Victoria') had been raised by Millet[3]. However, in 1878 in a French horticultural periodical, it was mentioned as having come from Britain, the assumption being that it was George Lee's cultivar, 'Victoria Regina', and James Backhouse and Son Ltd of York noted in their catalogue that they considered it to be quite distinct from Lee's 'Victoria Regina'. The flowers of 'Czar Bleu' were described as a beautiful shade of blue, abundantly produced in the spring, but without the substance of other sorts. It was grown for cut-flower work near Grasse and was included in at least one English catalogue as 'Blue Czar' which may account for 'The Czar' sometimes being listed as 'Purple Czar', presumably to try to prevent further confusion.

In 1884, Millet introduced the Parma violet 'Madame Millet' which had been raised by M.Néant of Bièvres in 1868. This new break in colour, rosy heliotrope (sometimes rather variable, see Chapter 5), was thought to have been a seedling and was awarded a certificate by the Paris Horticultural Society in 1875. Assertions by Roy Genders[4] and Georgianne Giffen[5] that this cultivar was raised by Millet are in conflict with contemporary French accounts.[6]

The origins of 'Princesse de Galles' are also rather confused, this being the violet usually grown in Britain as 'Princess of Wales'. Roy Genders stated that it was first sent out from Windsor Castle,[7] but again, this seems to run contrary to contemporary accounts and therefore, in line with current botanical practice, this cultivar has been referred to throughout this book as 'Princesse de Galles'. Bunyard mentioned that although this cultivar was raised by Millet, he gave away one of the first plants and this was multiplied and offered for sale in the south of France. It was mentioned in *L'Horticulteur Belge* in 1898 that this cultivar was a seedling of 'Gloire de Bourg-la-Reine' and had been raised in 1889. Four years earlier, the same periodical announced that 'Princesse de Galles' had been introduced by de Morin, while Paul Granger wrote that it had been found in a bed of 'The Czar' in 1888.[8] Owen Thomas, a frequent contributor on violets to *Gardeners Chronicle*, stated in the 27 September 1902 issue that it had been introduced from Hyères a few years before.

Henry Cannell had acquired plants by September 1896 and sent some blooms to the editor of the *Journal of Horticulture and Home Farmer*; in the following March it was described in that periodical as being the finest of all singles with flowers as large as a florin (10p piece). Flowers up to 5 cm (2 in) across have been recorded at the Windward Violet Nurseries and, at The Violet Farm, Corfe Mullen, flower stems between 30 and 40 cm (12 and 16 in) long were not uncommon. This cultivar was, however, among the most prone to red spider mite and aphis infestations and the serious outbreak of the latter at Dawlish and Holcombe in the 1930s mainly affected this cultivar (see also Chapter 9). In the USA as well as in England, 'Princesse de Galles' became the most popular scented single cultivar and as early as 1902, George Saltford was writing that tens of thousands of plants of this cultivar were being grown there.

'La Luxonne' or 'Luxonne' was another leading cultivar in France and although its origins are not well documented, Millet has been credited with having raised it, allegedly by crossing 'Wilson' and 'The Czar', the same parentage as 'Gloire de Bourg-la-Reine' and probably 'Millet'. It was soon being grown on a very large scale in the south of France, where it had arrived in the Hyères area by 1888, and most of the bunches of violets sent to Paris and other towns and cities of northern France were of this cultivar. By 1899 it was being grown by Isaac House and Son at Westbury-on-Trym in England, and it was exhibited by them at the Kent Chrysanthemum Show in Margate on 8 November 1902. This cultivar had a marked resistance to attacks by red spider mite. It was also considered to be very hardy; for instance when being grown at W. Miles's violet farm at Ballydehob, Co. Cork, Ireland, it flowered from mid-October until mid-April, withstanding 12°F (–11°C) with impunity. In order to provide some idea of the free-flowering nature of 'Luxonne', John Weathers chose as an example Miles picking 7,000 blooms from a quarter-acre plot in one week when 14°F (–10°C) of frost were recorded one night and 7°F (–14°C) of frost on the following night.[9] In 1939 it was still the principal cultivar being grown commercially in the open at Stanton Harcourt, Oxfordshire.[10]

'Explorateur Dybowski', raised in 1893, was a very large, deep violet-mauve cultivar, the petals being rather narrow and having a metallic sheen. It was listed by several nurseries in Britain and in Germany at the beginning of the twentieth century. Mrs Grace L. Zambra wrote that it had been discarded at the Windward Violet Nurseries as it lacked scent and was inferior to 'Pamela Zambra', its seedling raised there. However, according to M. Millet, 'Explorateur Dybowski was sweetly scented. It was among the most resistant to red spider mite infestation.

Millet succeeded in improving upon near-perfection when he raised 'La France' to rival 'Princesse de Galles' and 'Gloire de Bourg-la-Reine', but there is some doubt as to which of these cultivars, both raised by Millet, was the seed parent. The flowers of 'La France' were about the same size as those of 'Princesse de Galles' under ordinary conditions, but with special attention they could be larger. In colour, as James C. House commented, they were two shades darker than 'Princesse de Galles' and also had a metallic sheen. The flowers were carried on somewhat shorter stems, although still ample for bunching. In areas which suited this cultivar it was freer-flowering and hardier and the habit was more compact which could be an advantage under glass. The Misses Allen-Brown wrote that this cultivar, according to information they had, could not be grown in Cornwall;[11] however, it was recommended by the Ministry of Agriculture, and a qualification would surely have been given if it always failed in one of the most important violet-growing counties in England. It was also being grown at the Experimental Horticultural Station at Rosewarne, near Camborne. One can assume that as 'La France' could be temperamental, it had failed on some Cornish holdings, possibly as it was susceptible to red spider mite attack. It has been grown in the USA and South Africa.

Millet exhibited Ermanno Bredemeier's 'Principessa di Summunte' in 1899 at a meeting of the French National Horticultural Society and was awarded the First Class Certificate (see also pages 72 and 73).

In 1912 Millet raised 'Souvenir de Ma Fille', a cultivar with an even larger flower than that of 'La France'; it was the result of a cross between the multi-petalled giant cultivar 'Cyclope' and 'La France'. The French National Horticultural Society awarded it their Certificate of Merit on 26 February 1914. This cultivar had deep blue flowers with rounded petals which were somewhat waved. It was free-flowering, starting early in the season, and strongly scented. It was regarded as the best single cultivar growing at the Windward Violet Nurseries, although it was conceded that it needed good cultivation to give of its best, and this may have restricted its popularity as many British nurseries did not offer it for sale. It is still grown in France.

It is surprising how much controversy exists over the origins of many of the most famous of Millet's seedlings. In 1938, Mrs Grace L. Zambra wrote that 'Coeur d'Alsace' was 'a very old variety and not as so many people think a new hybrid'. Roy Genders shared this opinion as he wrote that it was a charming old cultivar,[12] while referring to the apparently older 'Souvenir de Ma Fille' as a new cultivar.[13] It is with some trepidation that the suggestion is made that both these distinguished writers could well have been wrong as the origins of 'Coeur d'Alsace' appear to be well documented; as Lionel Millet, writing in 1920 in *Revue Horticole*, recorded: 'During the war my father continued hybridizing his favourite flowers and crossed "Rubra" and "Le Lilas"; the result was "Coeur d'Alsace".' If one accepts that all three statements were made in good faith and were also accurate, the only solution is that the cultivar named 'Coeur d'Alsace' was not the violet (an old one) being described by the British writers. 'Coeur d'Alsace' was supposed to have flowers of medium size, produced freely and beginning early in the season. The colour was described as being unique, rose-purpurin, while that of the violet grown under the same name in Britain has a definite trace of salmon and is also quite distinct. Margery Fish wrote that it was 'a deep warm pink ... no wishy washy pale mauve tints'.[14]

It was awarded the French National Horticultural Society's Certificate of Merit on 12 February 1920, being described in *Revue Horticole* as a very remarkable new violet, and it has been grown widely in the UK and also in the USA.

The last Millet introduction to make an impact in the UK was the Parma violet, 'Président Poincaré' which was navy blue, a completely new colour in this type of violet, and which also had an extremely powerful perfume (see Chapter 5).

The nursery at Bourg-la-Reine was not restricted to violets; for instance, hellebore hybrids (Christmas and Lenten roses) were also specialized in. However, the collection of violets was probably the largest in the world, and this account, while mentioning most of the more important seedlings raised there, does not convey the size of their undertaking. One item that may help to place this in perspective is that, in the catalogue for 1914, at least four other novelties were included in addition to 'Souvenir de Ma Fille', these being 'Helvetia' (lilac), 'Mademoiselle Garridô' (rosy-lilac), 'Marietta' (mid-blue) and 'Rosea Delicatissima' (white with rose shading).

Armand Millet's book *Les Violettes: leurs origins, leurs cultures* (1898) was one of the first books written about violets by a specialist grower, and several articles on violets were published in French horticultural periodicals, many of which were by his son Lionel Millet.

The Royal Horticultural Society bestowed Awards of Merit on 'Princesse de Galles' and 'La France' (in 1895 and 1900 respectively) and only one other violet grower, John J. Kettle, has had the same awards made to two seedlings. It would seem that Royal Horticultural Society awards for violets have become progressively more difficult to obtain, as both 'Souvenir de Ma Fille' and 'Coeur d'Alsace' appear to have qualities that would make them potential award winners.

The range of violets grown would have been quite different but for the work of Armand and Lionel Millet, and there can be few other popular flowers where one hybridizer has so dominated its culture, as is the case with Armand Millet and the scented violet.

NOTES

1. E. J. Perfect, 'Russian Violets', *Journal of the Royal Horticultural Society* (October 1965).
2. Grace L. Zambra, *Violets for Garden and Market* (Collingridge, 1938).
3. E. A. Bunyard in *The New Flora and Silva* (1932).
4. Roy Genders, *Pansies, Violas and Violets* (Gifford, 1958).
5. N. Coon and G. Giffen, *The Complete Book of Violets* (Barnes, South Brunswick and New York, 1977).

6. E. A. Carrière, *Revue Horticole* (28 October 1875).

7. Roy Genders, *Collecting Hardy Plants for Interest and Profit* (Stanley Paul, 1959).

8. Paul Granger, *Fleurs du Midi* (Baillière, Paris, 1902).

9. John Weathers, *Commercial Gardening* (Gresham, 1913).

10. Ministry of Agriculture, Fisheries and Food, *Commercial Flower Production*, Bulletin (1939).

11. A. and D. Allen-Brown, *The Violet Book* (1st edn, Bodley Head, 1913).

12. Roy Genders, *Collecting Hardy Plants for Interest and Profit* (Stanley Paul, 1959).

13. Roy Genders, *Pansies, Violas and Violets* (Gifford, 1958).

14. Margery Fish, *An All the Year Round Garden* (Collingridge, 1958).

8
EARLY VIOLET FARMS AND NURSERIES

The following notes relate to some of the most famous violet growers, farms and nurseries which are mentioned elsewhere in this guide. There were many other establishments, which have not been included; well over 50 nurseries were selling violet plants in the UK during the 1930s and on many other holdings, violets for cut flower were an important crop. It is known that there were 150 acres of violets being grown in 1925; to these, Frederick Dillistone calculated, another 100 acres should be added, composed of plots on smallholdings.

It should not be thought that the commercial possibilities are restricted to bunched cut-flower and plant sales; Roy Genders wrote in 1957[1] of the potential of violet cultivation for the manufacture of perfume: 'In the south, large quantities of bloom are grown for the perfume industry, almost always under contract,' and further: 'Perfumed varieties ... are still grown in large quantities to supply the perfume industry in the making of soaps and scent, which like that of the lavender always retains its popularity.'

Genders also surveyed the production of violets for the cut flower trade: 'In Hampshire, Dorset, around the Dawlish area of Devon, and along the Falmouth–Penzance coastline of Cornwall, the bloom is grown for the London market and those of the other large towns of Britain.' This reinforces both Mrs Grace L. Zambra's comment made 20 years before: 'It is not at all an uncommon sight to see acres devoted to this one subject, especially in Kent, Sussex and Devonshire, where violets are largely grown for market,'[2] and that of Annie Garnett: 'Here in our own land, acres of ground covered with electrically heated frames, give work in plenty supplying those who sell flowers. The scent as one passes these fields is a delicious experience.'[3]

Turning for a moment to the non-commercial cultivation of violets, it is difficult to disagree with Mr Dillistone's claim that there was 'scarcely a private garden of any pretension that does not cultivate violets'.[4] Many indeed are the famous stately homes and country houses that are recorded as having had fine violets cultivated in the gardens, and the large-scale cultivation of violets in the royal gardens in this country and abroad is also on record.

Nevertheless, despite the present revival of interest in the violet, comparatively few nurseries stock them, which belies the importance of this flower in former years.

Early enthusiasts

R. W. Beachey, Devonshire. Probably the leading violet grower in Devonshire in the 1880s and 1890s, Beachey was growing 26 cultivars at Fluder on the boundary between Kingskerswell and Abbotskerswell near Newton Abbot in 1884 and he exhibited at the Torquay Show and others. He also wrote about violets.

Bunyard's Royal Nurseries, Maidstone Kent. These were famous for fruit trees and bushes (notable was the 'Allington Pippin' apple named after one of the firm's nurseries) as well as for seeds and herbaceous plants such as iris. Edward A. Bunyard wrote several articles about violets. A wide range of violet cultivars was listed until 1930 and at one time an acre of land, situated on the seed farm, was planted with violets.

Henry Cannell's Swanley Nurseries, Swanley, Kent. Two acres of violets were grown on this large general nursery and a considerable number of Parma violets were grown in pots. A very wide range of cultivars was offered for sale. Introductions included 'Blue and White', 'Swanley White' and 'Venice' – Parma violets, 'Empress' – hardy double and 'Rawson's White' – single. Violet growing probably ceased in about 1917.

Dillistone and Woodthorp, Munro Nursery, at various places including Sturmer, Haverhill, Suffolk and Braintree, Essex. They were a general nursery firm offering plants and bulbs. Nevertheless, violet growing was a speciality and generations of the Dillistone family grew violets for over 200 years. More than 20 cultivars were being listed as early as 1869. The hardy doubles 'King of Violets' and 'Queen of Violets' were introduced by this firm and the selection of 'Kaiser Wilhelm II', resistant to red spider mite, was selected by them. Frederick E. Dillistone gave at least two radio talks about violets and also wrote articles for periodicals, as well as a book *Violet Culture for Pleasure and Profit*. The firm was still selling violets in the late 1930s and many of the plants and bunches were carried, for the first part of their journey to customers, in a trailer behind Dillistone's bicycle. London hotels were among the customers for his violet flowers.

Isaac House and Son, Coombe Nurseries, Westbury-on-Trym. This firm of general nurserymen, fruit growers and market gardeners were formerly strawberry specialists. By the 1890s they had become famous for their violets and did much to popularize the new giant-flowered singles such as 'California' in Britain. Exhibits were staged at several shows, even as far away as Kent, and competitions were sponsored at the local Bristol Flower Show. The firm staged violet exhibits at 26 chrysanthemum shows in 1896. Several articles by James C. House appeared in the gardening press. An exhibit of Armand Millet's 'La France' received the Royal Horticultural Society's Award of Merit. Besides supplying their own customers, orders for violet plants taken by a nationally known firm of seedsmen (Suttons of Reading) were also dealt with. The firm in later years achieved fame as growers and raisers of *Scabiosa caucasica* (perennial scabious). Violets were probably discontinued after the nursery was sold for residential development in the 1930s, although James C. House did continue with scabious at Chew Magna in Somerset, later moving to Bristol where he was still offering scabious plants for sale in the mid-1950s as well as some small-flowered perennial asters.

Charles Turner, The Royal Nurseries, Slough, Buckinghamshire. The Parma violet 'Lady Hume Campbell' was introduced in 1875 and 'Wellsiana' in 1885. Twenty-six cultivars were still being offered for sale in 1935. The nursery also introduced many famous cultivars of other plants such as the 'Cox's Orange Pippin' apple and the 'Mrs Sinkins' border pink.

The Violet Farm, Corfe Mullen, Wimborne, Dorset, founded by John J. Kettle in 1905, enjoyed outstanding success when exhibiting at the Royal Horticultural Society shows where 24 medals were awarded between 1913 and 1932, as well as at Bournemouth, Southampton, etc. Besides the famous violets raised there (see Chapters 4, 5 and 7), the Parma violet 'Jamie Higgins' was introduced. Other introductions included the 'Lloyd George', 'Lord Lambourne' and 'Corfe Mullen Wonder' raspberries. Other flowers and fruit, as well as vegetables, were also grown. At its maximum extent the land amounted to about 100 acres (some used as farmland) with five 30-metre (100-foot) glass houses. At one time as many as 72 violet cultivars were being grown there. After the death of the founder in 1933, H. R. Jones and Son acquired the business and continued trading until 1968, offering quite a wide range of violet cultivars as well as other flowering plants and fruit canes and bushes. An article of mine about the farm and its founder was published in the *Journal of the Royal Horticultural Society* (see Bibliography).

The Violet Nurseries, Henfield, Sussex. Believed to have been founded in 1905, although this may refer to the year when the founders, a Miss A. Allen and a Miss D. Brown, decided to specialize in violets having previously grown a range of flowers. The rapid development of the nurseries is described in various books and articles (see bibliography). Over the years the range of plants was again extended and included glasshouse carnations and lavenders. Violet flowers and plants were supplied to customers at home and abroad and the nursery also produced and stocked many types of accessories utilising violets. For part of its existence, the nurseries trained horticultural students. The nursery side of the business closed down in 1952 with the site being acquired by Allwood Brothers of carnation and pink fame, and in different hands the sale of violet perfume ended in 1964. Several photographs of the nurseries survive and the Henfield Museum and the local history group ensure that this enterprise is not forgotten.

Thomas S. Ware, Tottenham, north London, and Feltham, Middlesex. A famous nurseryman who listed a comprehensive range of violets until *c*.1915. Ware introduced the famous single cultivar, 'The Czar'.

Windward Violet Nurseries, Holcombe, Dawlish, Devon, founded by George Zambra in 1922, offered for sale a wide range of cultivars, more than 60 in 1937 and still numbering 45 in the early 1960s when Windward was sold to Mr M. Ayres. Trading ceased within a couple of years. Violets introduced included 'Mrs R. Barton', 'Norah Church', 'Pamela Zambra' and 'Windward'. The Nurseries published a booklet *Violets, Simple Hints On How To Grow Them* by Mrs Grace L. Zambra, and her book *Violets for Garden and Market* is highly recommended. At one time violets were grown there on a considerable scale: between 7,000 and 10,000 plants of 'Princesse de Galles' alone were being planted annually in the 1930s. Other plants included *Iris germanica*, (following the death of the famous iris grower W. R. Dykes of Mayford, Woking, his collection was moved there), lavenders and *Nerine bowdenii*. The fact that several cultivars, such as 'Baronne Alice de Rothschild', 'California', 'Perle Rose', 'Kaiser Wilhelm II', 'Madame Noélie', 'Comte de Chambord' and 'Double Rose', were still being offered for sale in the late 1960s and early 1970s was the result of Mr and Mrs Zambra's dedication to the violet throughout much of their lives.

Notes

1. Roy Genders, *Pansies, Violas and Violets* (Gifford, 1958).
2. Grace L. Zambra, *Violets for Garden and Market* (Collingridge, 1938).
3. Annie Garnett, 'Violets through the Ages', *My Garden*, August 1936.
4. Frederick E. Dillistone, *Violet Culture for Pleasure and Profit*, (2nd edn, Benn, 1933).

9
CULTIVATION

Scented violets, large-flowered and small, in the full colour range from white, through shades of lilac, to bluish-violet, indigo, purple, magenta and rose, are either exclusively or in part descended from the wild sweet violet, *Viola odorata*, and are therefore hardy in Britain, with a few exceptions. The double forms of the single violet are also fully hardy, with the exception of Parma violet cultivars which are probably descended from another fragrant species native to warmer climes. At present, in England, violets are grown for cut flowers in Cornwall and Devon, and while excellent results can be obtained in the comparatively mild weather conditions prevailing there, flowers of similar quality can be grown elsewhere, having been produced commercially in Somerset, Dorset, Hampshire, Sussex, Kent, Surrey, Middlesex, Gloucestershire and Worcestershire.

During the nineteenth century the then widespread orchards (now mostly obliterated by the residential development of London's suburbs) were often underplanted with violets for the capital's flower markets. Most general nurseries, including those in Scotland and Ireland, have grown these plants, and commercial violet production in Co. Cork, with its similar climate to England's West Country, once appeared to have an important future (see page 15); so there is usually no geographical barrier to the cultivation of the violet in the United Kingdom and Ireland.

The effects of smoke pollution

It is important to remember, however, that in the past violets have usually failed near large towns and cities, regardless of their geographical location, unable to survive in the smoke-laden air. Violet growing in Middlesex succumbed probably because of the increasing industrialization of what were formerly small country towns, such as Staines, from which pollution would be carried by the prevailing winds to the violet plantations of Feltham, Hounslow and Isleworth. Nevertheless, violet growing close to London was not always an impossibility: Petts Wood and Bromley have been cited as favourable areas, while in December 1879, a large bed of violets in Battersea Park was attracting attention. A restricted range of cultivars was able to be grown in Croydon, even through the decades when pollution was at its worst and, according to one writer, they could be 'grown in absolute perfection in frames, not only within sound of Bow bells, but within sight of the Tower of London'.[1]

Failures did occur, however: notwithstanding the expenditure of a great deal of time and money in the early 1900s, an attempt to grow violets at Syon Park, the residence of the Duke of Northumberland, was unsuccessful despite its close proximity to the former important centre of violet cultivation at Isleworth.

Now, thanks to smoke control regulations, violet growing may again be possible in many places.

Hardiness

In the south and south-west of England, violets are rarely protected from the elements, other than from the wind on really exposed coastal sites, usually in Cornwall. Violets have been grown in the Dawlish area of Devon on sites adjoining the coast and thus without any adequate protection from the easterly winds which, after crossing Portland, are not broken by any land. Temperatures are quite mild there, but it does illustrate that cold winds, provided that they do not continue unabated for too long, need not be a barrier to violet cultivation, even if best avoided. Further north and east, the use of cloches and frames will result in the production of earlier flowers, free from possible weather damage; but except in the coldest districts, in any but the most severe winters, there is little risk of the plants being destroyed. The choice of the hardiest cultivars can make violet growing possible almost anywhere.

Growing conditions

Violets are often seen spreading over quite large areas in older and neglected gardens, where the exhausted soil will result in but a meagre return of flowers in relation to plant size; however, it does prove that if the violet can exist without attention, it will also succeed in the average flower border and so add beauty and fragrance at a time when the later flowering plants are in many cases just fresh green shoots. Edgings of compact sorts such as 'Lianne', or clumps of the larger cultivars such as 'California', are worthy of a trial in almost any garden. In rock gardens, a drift of 'Sulfurea' with apricot and cream flowers set against deep green foliage, or a few plants of the almost unforgettable 'Double Rose' can add a different kind of beauty when most of the other blossom is from bulbous subjects.

PREPARATION – GETTING THE CONDITIONS RIGHT
Although violets can survive in unfavourable conditions, to obtain satisfactory results the choice of a site and its subsequent preparation will need to be

carefully undertaken. Wild violets flourish in clay and chalk areas, but in both cases the plants are usually in hedgerows where their roots are near the surface in moist leaf mould. If the actual soil is reached, it will usually be only the substantially enriched topsoil, rather than the typical soil of the area in which at first glance the violets might have been thought to be growing.

Site To match the conditions in which violets thrive, these should be cool, reasonably moist situations in partial shade. South-facing borders allow the maximum amount of sunlight to ripen the crowns and so, according to some growers, increase the number of flowers later. This is probably sound advice, but these conditions will also favour the red spider mite once the topsoil becomes dry; and if the situation becomes really warm in summer, the plants will flag, and aphids, another serious pest, will be encountered unless watering is carried out.

Soil Provided that the would-be grower can distinguish between water-retentive soils which are desirable, and badly drained soils which in an untreated state are harmful to violets, the actual condition of the soil is less important. However, shallow soils will not produce the best violets as the root system will delve in ideal conditions 30 cm (12 in) or more down into the earth; likewise, even if the soil is deep it must be worked deeply and thoroughly so that the roots can penetrate it easily. The acidity or alkanity of the soil should be corrected well in advance of planting. Very acid soils will not produce good violets and while alkaline soils are preferred, if the alkalinity is too high, chlorosis will occur, slowing up growth and possibly masking disease or virus symptoms. The soil will need to be well broken down and in the case of heavy clay soils, cultivation should not take place when these soils are very wet, lest the soil structure is harmed, which will then make waterlogging likely. A dressing of general-purpose fertilizer should be applied at least two weeks before planting and as the violet thrives where there is plenty of humus in the soil, this can, if necessary, be added in the form of well-rotted leaf mould, composted plant material, etc., well in advance of planting. Care must be taken to see that these materials do not adversely affect the acidity of the soil, and in the case of leaf mould, it should be remembered that wireworms and other soil pests may be present within it. These must be eliminated prior to planting.

Moisture levels Ideally the soil should remain reasonably moist in summer, but it must not become waterlogged after heavy rain: although the violet likes moisture, an excess will cause diseases to become rife and if the land is waterlogged for some time, root rots become increasingly likely. A good **air circulation** should also be aimed at by regular weeding and by adequate spacing of the plants; this, together with a well-drained site, will probably lessen the incidence of diseases; with the violet as with other plants, time spent at the planning stage will be more than compensated for by later savings in time, labour and money.

WEEDS

The choice of site is one of the most important aspects of violet cultivation. The presence of vigorous weed growth will often indicate a fertile site with plenty of humus where violets should do well, but perennial weeds such as creeping thistle and couch grass must be eradicated as they will compete for light and nutrients. This should be done prior to planting as attempts to remove them later by hand will disturb the violets' root systems and cause a setback to growth. The avoidance of manual or chemical intervention, and the provision of natural conditions as far as possible will give the best results.

Hoeing should be undertaken regularly as the plants grow, to create a tilth and thus help to retain the soil moisture, as well as prevent the establishment of weeds. A fortnight or so later, hoeing should be repeated even if no weeds have appeared. If large numbers of plants are being grown, a wheel hoe can save time, but if the blades are set too finely, damage to the roots of the violets close to the surface may occur. In order to avoid this, a short-handled onion hoe should be used near the plants.

TREATING THE SOIL

Top dressings can be applied, but whether these will be of lasting benefit is doubtful as the aim should always be to provide sufficient plant food in the original base dressing. Well-weathered soot is often used as a top dressing and this may deter red spider mites. (There are, however, other methods of dealing with this pest; see also page 105)

Runners will be produced as the summer advances; the numbers will depend very much on the choice of cultivars, as will also the length of the actual runners. 'The Czar' and 'Amiral Avellan' are examples of cultivars that produce many runners, while the runners produced by giant-flowering violets such as 'Askania' are very long. 'Lianne' and 'La Violette des Quatre Saisons' are examples of violets producing very short runners, which are best described as offsets. All runners should be removed directly they are seen, to concentrate all the strength of the plant into the developing crown; and the flowers will be of better quality, come earlier and be carried on longer footstalks. Hoeing, watering, spraying (discussed in this chapter) and derunnering should be carried out throughout the summer when necessary. Derunnering should be discontinued from late summer, which will help to increase the frost resistance of the plants.

PLANTING VIOLET RUNNERS

Violets can be obtained as rooted runners or planted in flower pots for much of the year, while alternatively, large clumps of some cultivars are offered for sale in the autumn and are intended for almost immediate flowering under glass. Large clumps purchased in the autumn will of course cost more than runners acquired earlier and grown in the garden all summer. Runners should be planted up to 45 cm (18 in) apart, the exact distance depending on the vigour of the selected cultivar. When planting takes place, it is essential to dig the hole deep enough to accommodate the root system without doubling it up; otherwise a setback to growth will occur. The runner must be firmly planted with its crown at soil level. The crown is the part from which the leaf stalks arise and no part of any leaf stalk should be under the soil. A trowel should be used when planting runners on a small scale; a dibber can be used but if the soil is at all compacted, it can be hard work. If the soil is dry or if hot weather is forecast in the next day or two, the runners should be watered in, this ideally being done late in the day if hot weather comes before planting is complete.

PICKING THE FLOWERS

Flower buds will be observed on some cultivars as autumn approaches. All the flowers should be picked (unless the plants are intended solely for garden decoration) as this will result in a greater quantity of flowers being produced. The correct time to pick the flower is immediately maximum size has been attained; once picked, unlike some other flowers, those of the violet will not continue to develop. Flowers picked in the early morning will usually last the longest; failing this, picking should be undertaken in the evening. When grown commercially, the violets should be stood in water for a while after bunching, before being packed in boxes for the journey to the markets.

Propagation

Violets are usually propagated after flowering has taken place and the young plants will thus commence growth before the hot weather of the following summer.

Layering Cultivars that produce long runners are usually layered. The procedure is to leave runners on plants that are considered to be the most healthy and typical of the cultivar. When the runners are long enough, that is when a crown is developing at the end of the runner, and it is large enough to handle, all leaves except at the crown should be removed and the length of stem thus exposed between this crown and the parent plant should be buried under the soil. If the weather is dry, watering may be necessary to encourage the formation of roots along the runner, but this should be withheld for a day or two after the runner is buried. The crown will of course continue to receive sustenance from the parent plant. A strong root system should have formed after a few weeks have elapsed and when its presence has been ascertained by careful removal of some of the soil covering, the runner should be severed close to the parent plant. Frequent watering will then be necessary in dry weather until the root systems of the layers become self-supporting. After a few more weeks, the young plants can be transplanted either to the place where they are intended to flower, or to another bed for growing on.

This process can be carried out in the autumn; layers heeled in through the winter will give early planting material in the following spring, but this may result in the quality and quantity of flowers produced by the parent plants being adversely affected.

Division In the case of cultivars that either do not produce runners or only very short ones, division of the clumps will have to be undertaken after flowering, in place of layering. It is usual to leave two or three young crowns on each division and, as is the case when dividing other hardy perennial plants, the older parts of the clumps should be discarded and burned. Many violets can be propagated from seed, but there are three disadvantages to this method of propagation: firstly, it is not certain that the seedlings will closely resemble the parent, although of course this can be a source of interest as distinct forms may arise; secondly, as a rule, the larger the flower of a scented violet cultivar, the less likely that cultivar is to set seed; and thirdly, unless ripe seed is sown directly after harvesting, it will not germinate quickly and many months may elapse before the seedlings appear. (In the case of seed that has been stored, exposure to frost of the container may serve to accelerate germination.)

PESTS

Although most failures in violet growing are probably caused by poor cultivation, pests and diseases are capable of inflicting severe damage. The chances of this will be much reduced if the initial stock is obtained from a reliable source; and if these plants can then be grown on steadily, troubles will be less likely to occur.

Eelworms can cause the most concern as there is no certain method that the small-scale grower can use to eradicate them from infested stock, and care must be taken not to transplant infested violets to unaffected ground and spread the problem. Eelworms travel in the soil moisture and will thus tend to spread downhill where there is a slope and the spread will be worse in a wet year than in a drier one. The traditional method of dealing with this pest on many different plants has been the hot water treatment, during which the infested plants are immersed in very hot water for a stipulated length of time.

Theoretically, if the water is maintained at the correct temperature, the eelworms will be killed and the plants, or most of them, will survive and can then be planted out on eelworm-free land. However, if the water is not hot enough, these pests will survive and if too hot, both the plants and the eelworms will be killed; the use of a reliable thermometer, or preferably two, is therefore vital.

More research has been carried out regarding hot water treatment of, say, narcissi and chrysanthemums than has been done with violets, but it would seem that violets are more easily damaged by this treatment than other crops. Fortunately, eelworm attacks on violets are much less common, but vigilance is nevertheless essential, especially if plants are being grown in large numbers. And inadequate crop rotation is likely to allow eelworm to thrive, as well as resulting in a build-up of nutrients in the soil of which violets make little use.

The insecticide, Nicotine, has been thought to have some effect in controlling eelworms present outside the plant tissue, while some systematic insecticides are known to be capable of destroying eelworms (nematodes).

The symptoms of the presence of this pest are swellings on the runners, foliage and roots. If eelworm damage is spotted, it is best that all infested plants be dug up, complete with their roots and as much of the soil directly in contact with the roots as possible, with, as a precaution, the plants immediately adjoining the infested ones; all these plants should be burnt. The gaps thus created in the rows must not be replanted.

It is important to distinguish between the symptoms of eelworm and those of midge larvae. In the case of the latter a midge lays eggs on leaves and these roll up around the larvae and become swollen. This is a less serious pest, and if dealt with promptly, should not warrant severe measures. It can be controlled by spraying with derris, pyrethrum or other insecticides, but non-systemic (contact) insecticides will not reach larvae within the rolled up leaves. These leaves should be removed directly they are seen, and burnt.

Red spider mites can be a significant pest, especially in a hot, dry summer. These mites are orange and are almost too small to be seen without a microscope. The damage they cause results in the foliage appearing to be scorched or mottled due to the undersides of the leaves having been eaten, although not deeply enough to cause holes. Liquid derris will reduce the infestation, as will forcibly spraying the foliage, particularly the undersides, with water at normal temperature. Regular watering of the plants in dry weather will eliminate the conditions in which the mites thrive. Some scented cultivars have shown a resistance to attack, for example 'Baronne Alice de Rothschild', 'California', 'Christmas', 'Explorateur Dybowski', 'Kaiser Wilhelm II', 'Lianne', 'L'Inépuisable', 'Luxonne', 'Madame Noélie' and 'White Czar'. However, no scented cultivars are completely immune and some, especially 'La France', 'Madame Schwartz' and 'Princesse de Galles', have been regarded as very susceptible. Unscented cultivars such as 'Governor Herrick' and the fleetingly scented 'Pamela Zambra' owe much of their popularity to being almost totally immune to attacks by this pest, a characteristic being inherited from *Viola cucullata* and similar scented American species.

Modern acaracides will destroy this pest, although some of them are unsuitable for amateur use; likewise, on a larger scale a biological control can be tried by introducing insect predators of the red spider mite, but if another pest occurs in troublesome numbers and spraying is resorted to, the red spider mite predators will also be destroyed. The application of derris or water as mentioned earlier, and the avoidance of planting in hot dry sites such as at the foot of a south-facing wall, will probably be sufficient preventive action in ordinary gardens.

Greenfly (aphis) can cause serious problems by congregating on the buds and foliage and feeding on the sap. These attacks will directly result in distortion and general debility; moreover, sap will be carried from one plant to another, so should a plant be infected by a virus, this will be transmitted to the next plant or plants visited by a greenfly and an entire bed of violets can succumb very quickly by this means.

During the 1930s, a severe infestation of greenfly struck the violet farms around Dawlish, and it was thought that a previously unknown species was involved. It is not known when it first arrived in the area, but it attracted attention in the 1931–32 season when six acres of plants were almost completely destroyed, involving one grower in a loss of £200 and another of £130, considerable amounts of money in those days. The cultivar 'Princesse de Galles' appeared to be the most susceptible. Losses were even worse in the 1932–33 season, but in the seasons of 1933–34 and 1934–35, some growers dipped every runner in insecticide or soap and water prior to planting, and avoided the infestations. Symptoms of the damage resembled those caused by the small leaf **virus** that attacks strawberries, so it is likely that a virus was responsible for the severe losses among these violets.

There is no cure for virus-infected violet plants and so they should be burnt, along with those immediately adjoining. Symptoms include distortion of flowers and foliage, light patches on the foliage (sometimes almost invisible, sometimes resembling a variegation) and a general decline in the vigour of the plants. Care must be taken not to confuse these symptoms with those directly caused by greenfly and other pests, and also chlorosis induced by trace element and other deficiencies often on soils that are too alkaline. Dipping newly purchased runners in derris solution prior to planting will help to prevent the introduction of various pests and provided the plants are sprayed at the first sign of greenfly infestation, virus infection is unlikely. Derris and pyrethrum insecticides contain the naturally occurring substance rotenone, which will not only control greenfly and thus reduce the risk of virus attack by destroying the carrier or vector, but will also, as mentioned earlier, partially control red spider mites too. There is no record of greenfly developing strains that are resistant to these sprays, as was the case with DDT and other similar chlorinated hydrocarbon insecticides. There was also some evidence that DDT was destroying naturally occurring predators of red spider mites and having no control at all over the red spider mites, thus resulting in an even worse infestation.

Derris and pyrethrum are comparatively harmless to warm-blooded animals when used in accordance with the manufacturers' directions, but are fatal to cold-blooded creatures, so fish and reptiles could be unwittingly destroyed by their use.

OTHER PESTS
Soil pests such as **wireworms** and **millipedes** (though not centipedes which are very effective predators upon pests) will cause a certain amount of damage, but in the average well-cultivated garden, this will be insufficient to warrant specific measures being taken to control them. However the position is quite different when possibly infested leaf mould is being added to the soil or when grassland is newly cultivated, as very great losses will occur when planting is carried out where these pests are present in large numbers. Fungus diseases will be rare on sites where there is adequate air movement and drainage.

VIOLETS UNDER GLASS
When violets are grown under glass, it must be remembered that the plant is hardy and does not thrive in high temperatures, so ample ventilation will be necessary in all but the coldest weather. In the comparatively mild conditions under glass, greenfly will remain active and spraying or fumigating may become necessary in winter to control them. Red spider mites thrive when insufficient moisture is present, and if necessary the foliage should be sprayed with water to prevent a build-up of this pest. The plants will be more susceptible to disease attack than in the open, hence the necessity for good ventilation so that the foliage can dry out between waterings. Violet plants that have been forced are not usually considered as being suitable material for propagation.

Parma violets

The notes given in this chapter will apply in most instances also to the cultivation of Parma violets, but there will be a few differences because they originate from the Mediterranean area and are not hardy in any but the mildest parts of the British Isles and the USA. Even in favoured areas where the plants would be at no great risk in winter, the quality of the flowers would be reduced without protection and the Parma violet's property of flowering continually all through the winter would be lost.

PROPAGATION OF PARMA VIOLETS

Propagation of Parma violets should be carried out in the autumn. Runners should have been removed as soon as possible and then discarded throughout the summer so that the strength of the plants is concentrated on the future flowering crowns. However, as autumn approaches, an even shorter, stockier type of runner will be observed; these should be detached from healthy plants and planted a few inches apart in a well-prepared bed. Rooting will be swift, indeed some roots may even be seen when the runner is removed from the parent plant. Overwintered under cloches or in a frame, they will be ready for planting out in April or May at about 25 cm (10 in) apart.

CARE UNDER GLASS OF PARMA VIOLETS

The parent plants should be tended as described for singles earlier in this chapter. Ventilation should be provided whenever possible and the frame lights might need covering with matting in really cold weather. Looking back to the cold winter of 1977–78, I supplied bunches of blossom all winter except in the coldest spell which lasted for about two weeks, and the reason for the lack of flowers then was that to have handled the frozen glass or polythene would have caused it to crack or tear; the flowers remained undamaged and were eventually picked and bunched, when the holding frost had thawed. Even if the flowers are not required for decoration, they must still be picked when they die to prevent rotting, as the spores could spread to the buds and young leaves.

IN THE USA

In the United States, the violets occupied the violet houses for all but about two months of the year and propagation took place just as flowering was ending in April. The use of young crown runners similar to those recommended for autumn propagation, sometimes already partly rooted, grown on for a few weeks in beds of clean sharp sand, was standard practice while the soil in the houses was laboriously changed, in an attempt to prevent pests and diseases from being carried over on to the new plantings.

The problems encountered by the growers there have been mentioned (see pages 69 and 70) and now glasshouse Parma violet production has all but ceased, but an interesting legacy of photographs reproduced in books by George Saltford, Beverley Galloway and Nelson Coon remain, as does the name 'violet farm' used there now by growers of Saintpaulias (South African 'Violets'). I doubt whether an amateur, regardless of cost, could spend sufficient time to ensure the wellbeing of a violet house today, and for the commercial grower the returns from a year-round occupation of houses by violets must be compared with a cropping system of, say, summer tomatoes followed by winter lettuce in the same glasshouse.

However, autumn propagation has real possibilities and it has stood the test of time, having been used for the cultivars 'Lady Hume Campbell' and 'Marie Louise' for many years at Windsor (a reference to John Dunn's account of violet growing there will be found in the Bibliography). The violet plants stay healthy, having longer to develop than those from late winter or early spring, which seem to have no advantages beside a saving of space. Division of the old plants is often advocated and, provided only the vigorous young material is retained, this can be successful. It should be noted that the planting of several Parma crowns in one hole is often advised, but I believe this would seem to indicate the use of an inferior stock, or what amounts to an admission that crown runners struck later than the autumn have insufficient time to mature fully before the flowering season begins. Certainly autumn-struck crown runners should fill the space adequately when planted separately.

The use of the autumn-struck runners does mean extra space having to be found for them through the winter, but they will suffer no setback should the following summer prove to be dry. I suggest the planting-up of permanent frames with melons or cucumbers after the violets have been moved, the transference of cloches to cucumbers or peppers and planting tomatoes in a glasshouse if it has been used for violets. First-rate Parma violets should result, with flowers an inch or more across often on 2.5-cm (8-in) stems – and there will be the produce from the other crops as a bonus.

NOTE
1. M. Hampden, *Town Gardening* (Thornton Butterworth, 1921).

BIBLIOGRAPHY

Books on the subject of violet growing have been published in the USA over the years, and there have been articles in the periodicals of the Royal Horticultural Society, but when this book was first published in 1981, no British book entirely devoted to violets had been published since 1938 and no revised edition of an earlier work had been published since 1950. Nothing had been published for over 20 years that had dealt at length with violet growing. The dearth of modern works therefore gave increased importance to earlier publications. Since 1981 not only have additional books and articles appeared but additional older publications have been traced. The following annotated list contains most books and some articles that have been published about the history and cultivation of scented violets in the United Kingdom and the USA.

Abbiss, H. W. *Commercial Violet Production* (Cornwall County Council Education Committee, 1938). A reprint of a series of articles first published in *The Market Grower and Salesman and Fruit Trader*.
The author was Horticultural Superintendent for Cornwall, England, where he was instrumental in developing the violet trials at the Rosewarne Experimental Horticultural Station near Camborne. He had previously held a similar position in Devon during the time when violet production there was beginning to increase rapidly. This booklet contains information on violet cultivation in the West Country. The advisory leaflets about violets published by the Ministry of Agriculture, Fisheries and Food were probably based on this work.

Allen-Brown, A. and D. *The Violet Book* (The Bodley Head, 1913) 109pp.; 2nd edn (Taunton, Somerset: Barnicott and Pearce, The Wessex Press, 1922) 94pp.; 3rd edn (The Wessex Press, 1926) 94pp.
The authors ran The Violet Nurseries, Henfield, Sussex, England, and research by the Henfield Museum suggests with near certainty that the authors were a Miss Allen and a Miss Brown. The illustrations by Irene M. Johns are of an exceptionally high standard and depict six single cultivars and four Parma cultivars all in colour. The text provides a descriptive account of The Violet Nurseries and of violet cultivation in general. There are other illustrations. The second edition contains a continuation of the history of The Violet Nurseries dated 1921, but in fact ending with the Armistice in 1918. Several revisions have been made throughout the edition. The third edition is disappointing to the historian as, apart from the correction of a few printing errors, the text is exactly the same as that of the second edition

which was, as already mentioned, three or four years out of date when published. The only change in this cheaper (as described in The Violet Nurseries catalogue) edition, apart from the covers being coloured violet instead of green, was that all but one of the plates were excluded and no new ones added.

—*Violet Culture* (Cable Printing and Publishing Co. Ltd, *c.*1909), 59pp.
The forerunner of the above, an excellent cultural handbook, brief but to the point. Fifteen line drawings by H. L. Milne depict scenes at The Violet Nurseries and aspects of cultivation.

Amato, Mia 'Marketing Cut Violets in the US', *Sweet Times*, Spring 1996, pp.7, 16.
The geographical scope is wider than implied by the title.

American Rock Garden Society *Bulletin of the American Rock Garden Society,* Vol. 4, No. 6 November–December 1946, 'Our Violet Number', 23pp.
Contains several articles and notes mainly on violet species growing both in the wild and in gardens in the USA.

Appleyard, Angela 'Violet Farming', *The Farmer and Stock-Breeder Special Supplement*, 4 January 1938.
Mainly about the Windward Violet Nurseries, and illustrations include one of Mrs Grace L. Zambra.

Arnot, Jean 'Windward Violet Farm Dawlish Devon 1922–1961, 1980–1984', *Sweet Times,* Winter 1996, p.10.
Although the business first ceased to trade later than 1961, this is a definitive account of the revival during the years 1980–84 by one of Windward's owners.

Bailey, L. H. 'A Local Florist' (How to make a living from the land. XII), *Country Life in America*, April 1905, commences p.672.
A description of the Saltford business, in New York State, which had recently ceased growing violets. The centre of violet cultivation was moving from Poughkeepsie to Rhinebeck.

Barandou, Pierre 'The House of Barandou', *Sweet Times,* Winter 1995, pp.3–4.
This French violet grower traces the development of his horticultural business.

—'The Toulouse Violet among the Traditional Orders', *Sweet Times* Summer/Fall 1998, pp.3–4.
Traces the history of Parma violets with particular emphasis on the Toulouse area. Excerpts from an article prepared for a German magazine.

Bauer, Robert C. 'Village of Violets', *Ford Times*, February 1969.
A fairly brief account of past and then current violet growing at Rhinebeck, New York State.

Beachey, R. W. 'Violets', *The Journal of Horticulture and Home Farmer,* 25 September 1890.
A useful assessment of cultivars by the leading grower in Devon, England, at that time.

Bedoukian, Paul 'Vera Violetta (1892) by Roger and Gallet', *Sweet Times,* Summer 1996, pp.5, 15. First published in *Perfumer and Flavorist.*
Violet perfumes including formulae. Bibliography.

Beredjiklian, Norma 'Imperial Violets', *Sweet Times*, Summer 1994, pp.8–12.
The association of the violet with Continental European ruling families.

—'On the Road to Violet Wonderland', *Sweet Times,* Spring 1996, pp.13–16.
Edith and Emily Pawla, raisers of 'Royal Robe' and other violets, and their Pawla Violet Farm, Santa Cruz, California.

—'Violets in America and Doretta Klaber' *Sweet Times*, Fall 1995, p.5.
An assessment of Doretta Klaber's pioneering work *Violets in the United States*, 'a book that comes from the heart'.

Berlin, Barry 'Violets: Our Oldest Industry', *Rhinebeck Gazette*, 20 May 1965, pp.1, 9.
A review of past and then current violet growing. Includes a list of Rhinebeck violet growers (and the number of violet houses they cultivated) from a 1912 New York State florist growers' directory.

Boninti, Frances 'A Beginner's Guide to Seed Propagation', *Sweet Times*, Fall 1995, pp.11–12.
A detailed account.

Brett, W. *Pansies, Violas and Violets* (George Newnes, *c*.1927).

This information is taken from the title page. However, the front cover and spine carry a slightly different title: *Pansies and Violets*.
This useful general account, complete with line drawings and plates is one of the *How to Grow* series.

Brickell, Christopher and Sharman, Fay *The Vanishing Garden: a Conservation Guide to Garden Plants* (John Murray in association with the Royal Horticultural Society, 1986), 261pp. for pp.226, 228–231.
A useful brief history contrasting cultivar availability in the violet's heyday with various times since then.

Bunyard, Edward A. 'Among the Sweet Violets', *Gardeners Chronicle*, 23 April 1904.
The author, a leading violet grower in Kent, England, reviewed the cultivars he was then growing and so provided an interesting historical record.

—'The Violet, its History and Development', *The New Flora and Silva* Vol. 4 1936, pp.187–194.
A useful account with a critical review of some information in Armand Millet's *Les Violettes*.

Burbidge, F. W. *The Book of the Scented Garden* (John Lane, The Bodley Head Ltd, 1905), 96pp.
The author was Curator of Trinity College Botanical Gardens, and College Park, Dublin.
Plants including violets with comprehensive bibliography. One of the *Handbooks of Practical Gardening* series.

Burrows, Jean 'George Lee and his Clevedon Violets', *The Annals of Clevedon*, pp.1–5. (Clevedon Civic Society 1988.)

—'Lee's Legacy', *Newsletter*, National Council for the Conservation of Plants and Gardens Somerset and Avon Group, Spring 1987, pp.17–19.

—'Lovely Sweet Violets', *Area Newsletter*, National Association of Flower Arrangement Societies, Spring 1987, pp.28–31.

—'Vivat Victoria Regina', *The Garden: Journal of the Royal Horticultural Society*, May 1988, pp.239–241.
Includes an illustration of a selection of George Lee's violets by Yvonne Matthews. Reprinted without the colour illustration in *Sweet Times* Summer/Fall 1998, pp.9–10.

Carman, Kerry 'Little Charmers', *Listener* (New Zealand), 14 August 1999, p.50.
Includes illustration of Wylde Green Cottage Violet 'Covent Garden'. The interchange of violets between growers in various countries, where legally possible, has been a feature of the last 20 years. Kerry Carman raised the Wylde Green Cottage Violets and this and the following items include her own illustrations.

—'Locate, Identify and Record', *Listener and TV Times* (New Zealand), p.33.

—*Portrait of a Garden*, pp.249–252.

—'Potted Violets', *Listener* (New Zealand).

—'Sweet Violets', *The New Zealand Gardener*, August 1990, pp.52–55.

   'The Colour Purple', *Listener* (New Zealand), 26 June 1993, p.55.
Illustration of a mixed display of Wylde Green Cottage Violets 'in sweet profusion'.

—*The Creative Gardener* (1987), pp.105–108.

—'These Precious Old Hardy Double Violets ...', *Listener and TV Times* (New Zealand), 9 September 1991, p.37.
Illustrations of 'Mrs David Lloyd George' and hardy double violets, also Parma violets.

—'The Violet', *Listener and TV Times* (New Zealand), 2 September 1991, p.36.

—*Unfolding Seasons*, 1992, pp.14, 105–108.
Includes an illustration of Wylde Green Cottage Violets.

Casbas, Nathalie 'The Old Varieties of Violets that can be Found Again in France', *The Violet Society Journal*, Winter 1999, pp.4–5.
Successes in the search for 'lost' violets.

—'Those Wonderful Parma Violets', *The Violet Society Journal*, Spring 2000, p.4.
Parma violet cultivation in France with an emphasis on the Toulouse area, as well as a review of the cultivars.

Clarke, Charles J. L. 'Violet Farming', *The Windsor Magazine,* April 1908, pp.677–682.
The early years of what was then called The Henfield Violet Farm together with an account of everyday cultural practices. Ten illustrations from photographs by Messrs Clarke and Hyde of the violet farmers, the farm and various work in progress there, provide an almost unique record.

Clevedon Civic Society *The Annals of Clevedon,* 1988. Chapter One 'George Lee and his Clevedon Violets', pp.1–5, by Jean Burrows.

Coghill, Mrs Egerton 'The History of a Violet Farm', *Some Irish Industries; a Record of Contemporary Industrial Efforts in Ireland* (Dublin: *Irish Homestead* and The Irish Industries Association, 1897).
The author pioneered the development of the violet-farming industry in Ireland.

Cook, E. T. (ed.) *Sweet Violets and Pansies from Mountain and Plain* (*Country Life* and George Newnes, 1903), 100pp.
The section on Violet species begins on p.57, followed by Sweet Violets on p.83 and occupying the remainder of the book. Includes possibly the only surviving photograph taken at 'Mr. Heath's Nursery at Kingskerswell' (a frame of 'Comte de Brazza' Parma violets in bloom). The contents are mostly articles first published in *The Garden Magazine.*

Cook, H. H. 'The Cultivation of Violets', *Journal of the Royal Horticultural Society* (1932), pp.115–124.
The text of a lecture given at a RHS meeting in March that year. A useful record of violet cultivation with particular emphasis on cultural techniques and pests and diseases. H. H. Cook was a member of the staff of the University of Reading. Reprinted in *Sweet Times,* Fall 1993, pp.3–10.

Coombs, Roy E. 'Cultivated Violets: Are they really unscented?', *The Plantsman* (the Royal Horticultural Society quarterly), June 1981.
Intended as a rebuttal of Dr Miriam Rothschild's claim in a previous issue that cultivated violets were no longer scented.

—'John J. Kettle and the Corfe Mullen Violet Farm', *Journal of the Royal Horticultural Society,* May 1975, pp.210–214.
An account of the violet farm and of its founder.

—'Parma Violets', *The Plantsman* (the RHS quarterly), December 1979.

The history and cultivation of this class of violet.

—'Parma Violets', *Greenhouse*, October 1981, pp.39, 41.
The accompanying illustrations were of single-flowered, non-Parma
cultivars.

—'Some Hardy Double Violets of the Nineteenth Century', *Journal of the
Royal Horticultural Society*, September 1974, pp.400–404.
A chronological account.

—'Sweet Violets and How to Grow Them', *Amateur Gardening*, 20 April
1968.
A guide to scented single violets and their culture.

—'The Parma Violet "Marie Louise" ', *The Plantsman* (the RHS quarterly),
September 1982, pp.112–115.
Advancing the claim that red markings on flowers of supposed 'Marie
Louise' plants indicate the cultivar 'New York' and not 'Marie Louise'.

—'Vanishing Violets', *Amateur Gardening*, 29 June 1968.
One of the first accounts in which the risk of extinction facing many cultivars
was highlighted.

—'Violet Farming since Victorian Times', *Country Life* 15 January 1981,
pp.142, 147.
A brief historical account.

—'When Violets Grew (and Grew) in Dawlish', *Dawlish Gazette*,
19 June 1980.
The history and development of the violet farming industry in one of its
traditional centres in England.

—Material contributed to *The Magic Tree* (1989), see National Council for
the Conservation of Plants and Gardens Devon Group.

Coon, Nelson *Fragrant Violets, Their Care and Culture* (Rhinebeck Floral
Company).
At least three editions, the third being published in 1933. Unexamined.

—*Practical Violet Culture* (New York: De La Mare, 1925).
This has been described as the standard work on violets published in the
USA. It is as far as I can judge, error-free. The author concentrated on the

techniques used in the Rhinebeck area, so information about, for instance, violet growing in California and Massachusetts is lacking. There are more than 30 interesting and helpful illustrations of the violets, the violet houses and frames, bunching and packing, etc. It is an excellent guide. See also Galloway, *Commercial Violet Culture*.

—'The Fragrant Violets', see Kettle, *How to Grow Violets*.

—and Giffen, Georgianne *The Complete Book of Violets* (South Brunswick and New York: A. S. Barnes, 1977), 147pp.
Although there is a section on pansies, exhibition and bedding violas and violettas, most of the book is about violets and violet species. There are many excellent illustrations, some in colour, but in one case a carefully prepared exhibit of various cultivars lacks a key, and cultivar names are missing from other illustrations. Regrettably, the original publication is not always mentioned in connection with reproduced illustrations. Checklists of cultivars could have entries in greater detail and there are some surprising omissions and errors. The bibliography is lengthy, but the entries are unannotated, and again, there are some rather unexpected omissions. There is a section on the violet's medicinal uses and there are more recipes for the use of violets in cookery than in Mrs Grace L. Zambra's book, but there is little about violet perfume. It is a pity that these problems exist in a book, the title of which includes the word 'complete'. Notwithstanding these points, it was surely the finest book about cultivated violets in print when published.

Crane, D. B. Pansies, *Pansies and Violets* (W. H. & L. Collingridge, 1908).
Pp.88–105 include a general account of violet growing and a descriptive list of cultivars.

Crane, Howard H. *The Book of the Pansy, Viola and Violet* (The Bodley Head, 1908).
A general guide. The illustrations, reproduced from photographs of an exhibit of Isaac House and Son's violets at a flower show and of planting violets at their Coombe Nurseries at Westbury-on-Trym, England, are of particular interest, the latter being reproduced in this book. One of the *Handbooks of Practical Gardening* series.

Cuthbertson, William *Pansies, Violas and Violets* (Macmillan, 1898).
Contains details of culture, particularly of the picking and packing of the blooms for market. One of the titles in the *Dobbies Horticultural Handbooks* series (Dobbies being a leading Scottish horticultural establishment).

—Ed. *Pansies, Violas and Violets* (T. C. & E. C. Jack, 1912).
Pp.77–108 (out of a total of 116pp.) include a general account of violet
growing by R. H. Pearson, the series editor and also managing editor of
Gardeners Chronicle; a description of violet culture at Windsor Castle by
John Dunn who was in charge of that work; and notes on some of the
principal viola species by W. Irving. One of the *Present-day Gardening* series.

Davies, Jennifer 'The Victorian Flower Garden' (BBC Books, 1991), 240pp.
for pp.154, 156 and 159–161 (Chapter 12 'Mr Lee's Violets').
Accounts of techniques used in Victorian times, the Clevedon violet industry
and George Lee's role as well as the rediscovery of his violets by Jean
Burrows.

'Dawlish Violets Past History and Future Prospects', *Dawlish Gazette*, 30
January 1959. Extracts from Wilfrid C. Ibbett's article in January 1959 issue
of *Agriculture*.

di Brazza, Conte Luigi Savorgnin Cergneu 'The Violet – 'Conte Di Brazza',
The Violet Society Journal, Spring 2001, p.8.

Dictrich, Gregor 'Violets – A Case of Neglect', *The Violet Society Journal*,
Autumn 1999, pp.11–12, Winter 1999, p.11.
A translation of the updated text of an article first published in the Austrian
Garten periodical in 1996.

Dillistone, Frederick E. *Violet Culture for Pleasure and Profit* (Ernest Benn,
1926), 32pp, 2nd edn (1933) 62pp.
The author's family had grown violets for 200 years and his nurseries at
Sturmer in Suffolk, England, were one of the leading producers of violet
plants; this experience resulted in an excellent book dealing with violet
growing in this country and to a lesser extent abroad. All aspects seem to be
covered, especially the economics of the crop, although the historical
approach is somewhat limited. One of the *Practical Manuals for Market
Growers* series. Together with the article by Mr Bunyard in *The New Flora
and Silva*, one would have had an authoritative work at that time.

—'The Cult of the Violet', *Gardening Illustrated*, 5 July 1930.
An historical account of the violet's popularity.

Dunn, John 'Violet Growing at Windsor', see Cuthbertson, *Pansies, Violas
and Violets*.

Ellis, E. T. *The Garden* (Daily Express Publications) for section on Violets, pp.1139–40 by 'J.J.K.' (J. J. Kettle).

Fanin, Giulietto 'The Violet in Italy', *Sweet Times*, Summer/Fall 1998, pp.7–8.
Concentrates on the history of Parma violets.

Farrar, Elizabeth 'A Little History', *The Hardy Plant Society Viola Group Newsletter* Spring 1991. Republished in *Sweet Times* Winter 1992, pp.9–11.

—'On the subject of Violas, Violettas and Violets', *Sweet Times* Winter 1996, pp.13–14, 17.

—*Pansies, Violas and Sweet Violets* (Hurst, Berkshire: Hurst Village Publishing, 1989). Pp.32–62 (out of a total of 78pp.).

Gale, Val *Dawlish Violets: Some notes on the Dawlish Violet trade.* (Dawlish, Devon: Dawlish Museum).

—'Dawlish Violets for Queen Mary', *Sweet Times*, Winter 1996, pp.6–7.
A republication of much of the text of the above leaflet.

Galloway, Beverley T. *Commercial Violet Culture: A Treatise on Growing and Marketing of Violets for Profit* (De La Mare, 1899); 2nd edn (1903) 239pp.; 3rd edn (1914).
Nelson Coon, who made considerable reference to this work when preparing *Practical Violet Culture*, described it as 'thorough and thoughtful'. Many illustrations. Considerable detail on the economics of the crop and the building of violet houses.

Garibaldi, Don 'Italian Violets in California: The Story of the Garibaldi Family', *Sweet Times*, Spring 1996, p.9.
A history of the sole remaining commercial cut flower violet grower in the Western United States.

Garnett, Annie 'Violets through the Centuries', *My Garden*, August 1936, pp.591–593.

Genders, Roy *Collecting Antique Plants: the History and Culture of the Old Florists Flowers* (Pelham Books, 1971).
Includes a section on violets.

—*Collecting Hardy Plants for Interest and Profit* (Stanley Paul, 1959). Includes a section on violets.

—*Flower Growers Handbook* (Pearson, 1956).
Contains a section on violet growing for market and, by including details of the economics of the crop, it brought the relevant section of Frederick Dillistone's book up to date.

—*Pansies, Violas and Violets* (John Gifford, 1958).
Similar material to that in the above titles, but in rather more detail (the violet section being pp.142–183). It is doubtful whether many of the cultivars listed were commercially obtainable in the UK in the late 1950s and were probably extinct in 1971. Although difficulty and disappointment thus awaited readers hoping to obtain all the violets listed, these books do provide interesting reading. Roy Genders grew violets in Somerset. Also published in a Garden Book Club edition.

Godfrey, Blanche Lee *£100 a year from Parma Violets: A New Home Industry for the Man of Small Means* (Woodchester, Gloucestershire, 1928) 24pp., with an illustration of 'A Parma Violet Garden'.
Unexamined.

Greenoak, Francesca 'Shrinking Violets', *The Times*, 4 October 1986.

Griffiths, Mark 'Sweet Tenants of the Shade', *The Garden: Journal of the Royal Horticultural Society*, February 2001, pp.88–91.
Includes historical and cultural information as well as details of cultivars and stockists and further reading, including the booklet by Blanche Lee Godfrey.

Grindon, Leo 'The Violet', *Gardeners Chronicle*, 19 September 1974.
A guide to both the cultivation and the literature.

Groves, Clive 'A Dorset Violet Farm', *Sweet Times*, Spring 1998, p.8.
An historical account of Dorset's former leading violet farm at Corfe Mullen, England, and of its founder J. J. Kettle by the leading Dorset violet grower of today. The period covered is from 1905 until Mr Kettle's death in 1932, so the years when the farm was run by H. R. Jones and Son (until 1968) await description.

—'My Magical Violets', *Sweet Times*, Winter 1996, pp.11–12.
Recollections of the development of violet growing at the Bridport nurseries of C. W. Groves and Son.

'Growers find Violets gaining New Popularity', *New York Herald Tribune* 1 April 1940.
The then current situation in Red Hook and Rhinebeck.

Hardman, Mike 'A Violet by Another Name', *The Violet Society Journal* Autumn 2000, pp.6–7.
Plant classification and the early botanists.

—'Violet Plant Collections in the UK', *The Violet Society Journal* Winter 2000, pp.6–7.
A useful review.

Haynes, Ariel 'Violets: Surprising Variety from a Traditional Beauty', *Taunton's Fine Gardening* no. 24, March/April 1992, pp.54–57.
A review of violets and other violas.

Hearne, Richard 'The Cultivation of Violets' *The Monthly Pictorial*, January 1926.
About the Windward Violet Nurseries. Includes an aerial photograph.

Heath, J. *A Practical Treatise on Violet Cultivation* (Kendal, Westmoreland: Birkett, 1889).
A reprint of a series of articles first published in *Gardeners Chronicle*. The first book solely about violets to be published in England.

Hellyer, Arthur G. L. 'A Posy of Violets', *Financial Times*, 1972.
The author, a noted horticultural writer, was at one time employed by Isaac House and Son. An excellent article from both historical and cultural viewpoints.

—'Violets and Other Outcasts', *Financial Times*, 6 June 1981.
Partly a review of the first edition of this book. Also includes memories of violet growing and information on plant conservation, and the early years of the NCCPG.

Henslow, T. Geoffrey W. 'Sweet English Violets', *Morning Advertiser*, 17 October 1936. Republished in pamphlet form by the Henfield Violet Nurseries.
Unsurprisingly, the writer concentrated mainly on that establishment.

Hogan, Alice Mary 'Flowers Most Fragrant', *The Violet Society Journal* Summer 2000, p.5.
Violet growing in New York State.

House, James C. 'The New Giant Violets'. Articles on the new introductions of Armand Millet and others appeared in *Gardeners Chronicle*, 30 September 1899 and in *The Garden*, 6 January 1900.

—'Violets and their Cultivation', *Journal of the Royal Horticultural Society*, April 1917, pp.16–22. Republished in *Sweet Times* Summer 1993, pp.12–18. A good account of the history of many cultivars, and their evaluation by this famous Gloucestershire violet grower, still of interest. Text of lecture given on 27 March 1917.

Houston, Jourdan 'The Shrinking Violet Industry', *Horticulture*, March 1981, pp.20–23.
Although focusing on Rhinebeck, there are references to violets elsewhere and various literary sources outside the Hudson Valley are cited.

Ibbett, Wilfrid C. 'Dawlish Violets Past History and Future Prospects' *Agriculture*, January 1959. See also *Dawlish Gazette* 30 January 1959 and a separately published pamphlet.

Irving, W. 'The Genus Viola: Some of the Principal Species', see Cuthbertson, W. *Pansies, Violas and Violets*, 1912.

Johnstone, Katherine H. 'Growing Violets', *Journal of the Royal Horticultural Society*, September 1974.
The author was formerly Horticultural Adviser at Rosewarne Experimental Horticultural Station, Camborne, Cornwall, England. A valuable guide containing information on cultural techniques.

—See also Ministry of Agriculture, Fisheries and Food *Commercial Flower Production*.

Jones, George *Growing Together, a Gardening History of Geelong extending to Colac and Camperdown* (Australia). Includes information about John Raddenbury and the 'John Raddenbury' violet.

Kettle, John J. *How to grow Violets* (Wimborne, Dorset: The Violet Farm, Corfe Mullen), *c*.1933.
This posthumous booklet contains notes on the cultivation of single violets and there are also pages about 'The New Fragrant Violets' by Nelson Coon. The latter is mostly about the violet industry in the United States, but includes an evaluation of J. J. Kettle's work.

—See also Ellis, E. T. *The Garden* and Middleton and Marshall *Mr Middleton's Garden Book*.

Kimberley, Dorothy 'Growing Violets combined with full-time work', *The Hardy Plant Society Viola Group Newsletter*, No.2 Summer/Autumn 1991, pp.5, 6; Republished in *Sweet Times*, Winter 1996, p.17.
The development of the West Winds Nursery, Hereford, England.

Klaber, Doretta *Violets of the United States* (A. S. Barnes, 1976).
A superb reference work. Many coloured plates of exceptional quality by the author illustrate this detailed guide, the result of many years' endeavour, to wild violets throughout the country.

Laurie, A. and Poesch, G.H. *Commercial Flower Forcing* (Philadelphia; Blakiston, 1937)

Lee, George 'Lee's Victoria Regina Violet', *Journal of Horticulture and Cottage Gardener*, 26 February 1874.
The account of the discovery of the 'Victoria Regina' and 'Prince Consort' violets and of the raiser's hopes for further distinct seedlings.

—'Violets: Their Varieties and Culture', *The Florist and Pomologist* December 1873.
A very interesting article by the pioneer hybridizer and cut-flower grower.

Le Lievre, Audrey 'May Violets Spring', *Country Life*, 26 March 1998, pp.74–77.
A useful account with references to the International Violet Association. However, an excellent illustration of a Parma violet is wrongly captioned. There is a reference to the naming of the cultivar 'Princess Diana'.

—'Peer into a Purple Haze', *Country Life Gardens Special edition*, Summer 2001, pp.23–25.
An illustrated historical account.

Le Presley, Balfour 'My Great-Grandmother's Violets' *Sweet Times*, Fall 1996/Winter 1997, p.10.
The survival of a hardy double violet taken from England to Ontario, possibly as early as 1835, and which survived within a garden for at least 125 years.

Livingstone, A. E. 'Violets that Flower in Winter', *Amateur Gardening*, 22 May 1955.

Martin, Tovah 'And Violets are Blue', *Sweet Times*, Vol.1 No.2, pp.17–22.

—'A Return to Violets', *Victoria* June 1989. Republished in *Sweet Times* Vol.1 No.1, pp.3, 4.

—'It's Raining Violets', *The New York Times Pastimes*, 3 March 1991, p. 65. Reprinted in *Sweet Times*, Spring/Summer 1995, pp.6–7. Aspects of the violet's history and cultivation.

Mastrangelo, Dennis 'Picking Violets at Año Nuevo', *Sweet Times* Spring 1996, p.8. Description of the technique of picking and bunching violets in California.

Matthews, Yvonne 'Some Viola Species', *The Hardy Plant Society Viola Group Newsletter* No.5, March 1992, pp.2–5. Republished in *The Hardy Plant* Vol.15 No.2 Autumn 1993, pp.22–27.

'That Ordinary Old Violet', *The Hardy Plant Society Viola Group Newsletter* No.2, Summer/Autumn 1991, pp.2–4. Republished in *Sweet Times*, Winter 1996, p.15. A review of cultivars by the National Collection holder.

McCoy, Samuel D. 'Violet Village', *Woman's Day*, March 1955, starts on p.33. Violet growing at Rhinebeck: its history and then current trends.

McLeod, Judyth A. *The Book of Sweet Violets* (Australia: Wild Woodbine Studio). The section headings suggest a wide-ranging account. Unexamined.

Middleton, C. H. and Marshall, Captain *Mr Middleton's Garden Book* (*Daily Express* Publications, *c.*1930). This includes a section on violets by 'J.J.' (J. J. Kettle) in which he dealt with the general cultivation of the crop. Mr Middleton, the first BBC television gardener, was head gardener at Compton Acres in England and therefore had a Dorset connection with J. J. Kettle. The same material also appeared in another *Daily Express* publication *The Garden for Expert and Amateur*, edited by E. T. Ellis.

Ministry of Agriculture, Fisheries and Food *Violets* (Advisory Leaflet No.352, 1965). This leaflet should be consulted for details of commercial practice, and the relevant section in this and subsequent editions provides then up-to-date information on pest and disease control. Comparison with earlier editions, such as those of 1950 and 1956 (both entitled *Commercial Violet Growing*), reveals the trends taking place in the industry during that period.

—Commercial Flower Production Part 1 (1939). This Ministry bulletin by H. V. Taylor and K. H. Johnstone includes a detailed section on violets (pp.73–82) and two useful line drawings depicting runners suitable and unsuitable for propagation.

Moorman 'Those Shrinking Violets', an article from the 'Spade and Plough' feature in the *Clevedon Mercury*, 6 May 1983.
Includes an illustration of possibly the only surviving photograph, taken prior to 1914, of an exhibit of Clevedon (England) violets in their heyday. Also includes information on the Canter family who were leading violet growers in that area. Mrs Jean Canter has kindly allowed the photograph to be republished in this book.

National Council for the Conservation of Plants and Gardens Devon Group, *The Magic Tree: Devon Garden Plants History and Cultivation* (Exeter: Devon Books, 1989).
References to violets in three sections of the book (pp.24, 103–105, 162–163) combine to provide an account of violet growing mainly in the Dawlish area (England) with particular emphasis on the Windward Violet Nurseries, including its revival in the post-Zambra era.

Oldaker, Isaac 'On the Treatment of the Neapolitan Violets, so as to make them produce a Succession of Flowers through the Winter', *Transactions of the Horticultural Society,* April 1820. The text of a lecture read on 21 March in that year. Republished in *Sweet Times*, Vol. 1 No. 2 Spring 1993, pp.13–16.

Parry, Ernest J. *Cyclopaedia of Perfumery: a Handbook.* 2 vols (J. & A. Churchill, 1925).

Peace, Rob 'My Violet Collection' *The Violet Society Journal*, Winter 2000, pp.4–5.
The development of the national collection of violets in Australia.

Peplow, Elizabeth 'The Joys of Spring', *Amateur Gardening*, February 1980.

—'Scents for Spring', *Amateur Gardening*, 15 September 1979.

Both the above are short general accounts of violet cultivation.

Perfect, E. J. *Armand Millet and his Violets* (High Wycombe,
Buckinghamshire: Park Farm Press, 1996), 212pp. Pp.30–145 are an English
translation of Armand Millet's *Les Violettes, leurs origins, leurs cultures*,
published in France in 1898.
I mentioned in the first edition of this book that I considered Armand Millet's
work to be 'essential reading for anyone researching the history of violet
cultivation'. E. J. Perfect has done far more than translate as he has provided
detailed translator's notes and a biography of Armand Millet. Includes maps
and other illustrations, a few of which are from the original book.
Bibliography of Armand Millet's writings and a list of violet cultivars he
introduced. Pp.180–196 deal with tree violets.

—'Russian Violets', *Journal of the Royal Horticultural Society*, October
1965.
A detailed account of the development of single-flowered violets until the last
quarter of the nineteenth century. A brief cultural guide and a short reading
list are included. Excellent.

—'Tina Whitaker', *Sweet Times*, No.3 Summer 1993, pp.4–6.
The violet cultivar and the person after whom it was named.

Perry, Frances 'Sweet Violets', *Home Gardener*, 10 October 1964.
A useful account of violet cultivation for the amateur.

Pinney, Baldwin *Violets: Hints on how to grow them* (Kent 2nd edn, 1926).
The author ran the Marchurst Nursery and had displays of violets at major
exhibitions. He is particularly of note for popularizing the cultivar 'Tina
Whitaker'. Unexamined.

Pioli, Carlo 'Borsari 1870', *The Violet Society Journal*, Spring 2001, p.9.
The oldest perfumery company in Italy and Duchess Marie Louise's
involvement with Parma violets; her encouragement of the development of
the process for producing perfume as well as promotion of the colour Parma
violet.

Roberts, Sonia 'No Shrinking Violets', *Horticulture Week*, 12 December
1986, pp.24–25.
C. W. Groves and Son's Bridport nurseries with particular reference to
violets.

Robinson, Peter 'An Eden in the Garden of England: a Potted History of Henry Cannell and Sons of Swanley, Kent', *Sweet Times*, Winter 1996, pp.9, 12.

—'Roses are French Violets are English', *Sweet Times*, Winter 1996, pp.8–9. Violet growing mainly in the West of England.

Saltford, George *How to Make Money Growing Violets* (The Violet Culture Company, Brooklyn, New York, 1902).
The author pioneered violet growing in the Rhinebeck area. An excellent short guide with interesting illustrations of glasshouse production of violets there.

Saltford, Herb 'The Violet Revival', *House and Garden* (December 1940), pp.30, 50.
The violet's decline and then revival.

Sarsby, Jacqueline 'Shrine for Sweet Violets', *Farmers Weekly*, 23 March 2001.
Mainly about the Devon Violet Nursery, Rattery, South Brent, England.

—'Shrinking Violets' *Gardens Illustrated*, February 2003, pp.74–79.
Two of the remaining cut-flower violet enterprises in Cornwall, including the last at Feock.

—'The Gentle Violet', *Country Living*, May 2002.

—'Where have all the Violets gone?' *Daily Telegraph*, 19 May 2001.

Segre, Ada V. 'Historical Notes on the Sweet Violet' *The Violet Society Journal*, Spring 2001, pp.12–13.
Concentrates mainly on sixteenth and seventeenth centuries.

Taylor, H. V. See Ministry of Agriculture, Fisheries and Food.

'The Violet Industry: Poughkeepsie is the Center of Cultivation.'
Published in an unknown local newspaper in 1894. An historical account of the progress and setbacks of the violet-growing industry.

Thomas, W. H. *Little Points in Violet Culture* (Convent Station, New Jersey, 1902).
The text of a lecture read before the Morris County Gardeners and Florists

Society. The booklet would doubtless have been of help to those considering participation in the expanding violet industry.

Thorogood, Horace 'The Violet Coast', *Evening Standard*, 17 January 1938. Exploiting the violet industry's tourism potential in the Dawlish area of Devon.

Tucker, Arthur O. 'The Botanical Names of the Sweet Violet', *Sweet Times*, Fall 1995, p.5.
A useful account, including a bibliography with a rare reference to Judyth A. Mcleod's book.

—'Violets in Perfumery', *Sweet Times*, Summer 1996, p.4.
A wide-ranging account including artificial perfumes and other plants which have similar scents to that of the scented violet. Bibliography.

Walters, S. M. 'Observations on Varieties of Viola Odorata L.' (Arbroath, Scotland, T. Buncle, 1946).
Reprinted from the Report of the Botanical Exchange Club for 1943–44. Variations in wild forms of the sweet violet.

Ward, H. W. 'Cultivation of Violets under Glass', *Gardeners Chronicle*, 3 September 1881. A historical as well as practical account by the gardener in charge of violets at Longford Castle, Salisbury, Wiltshire, England.

Warner, H. H. 'Violets in Many Lands and Ages', *Gardening Illustrated*, 5 July 1930.
The definitive historical account.

Whitsey, Fred 'Purple Pros: Violets are shedding their "Granny" Image', *Daily Telegraph*, 8 April 2000.

Whittlesey, John 'Right Violet, Right Place', *Sweet Times*, Winter 1996, pp.16–17.
Violets for different planting positions in the garden as well as information on violet seedlings and the European Violet Gall Midge by the grower of probably the largest commercial range of violet cultivars in the USA.

Wilcox, Alfred 'Interview with a Violet Specialist. Mr J. J. Kettle, Corfe Mullen, Dorsetshire' *Garden Life*, 23 November 1912, pp.115–117.

Wilson, Helen Van Pelt *and* **Bell, Léonie** *The Fragrant Year* (Van Nostrand,

New York, 1967).
Contains an interesting section on violets. The British edition, published by
Dent, includes an additional chapter, by Graham Stuart Thomas.

Zambra, Grace L. 'Garden Violets' *Amateur Gardening,* 10 February 1940,
pp.63–64.

—'Violets' *The Guild Gardener,* November 1937, pp.170–171.

—'Violets for Fragrance' *Amateur Gardening,* 2 January 1951, p.10.

—*Violets for Garden and Market* (W. H. & L. Collingridge, 1938) 79pp; 2nd
ed. (1950) also 79pp but in a slightly different format.
All aspects of violet growing are covered, even recipes including violets. In
addition to a descriptive list of cultivars, there is also included a list of 'so-
called other varieties … which are all so similar to a variety already grown as
to be indistinguishable, even when grown side by side'. This list is highly
controversial as, although of potentially great use to the reader, it includes
cultivars such as 'Armandine Millet', 'Le Lilas', 'Luxonne', 'Wellsiana' and
'Wilson'. Cultivars such as these, often the first of their type, must be distinct
and therefore it should have been the later introductions, with which they
were considered apparently identical, that were included in the list. A
tremendous opportunity was therefore lost, particularly as the valid names
were not mentioned and the text was not amended in the second edition. The
main body of the text of the second edition, not having been rewritten or
revised (presumably as an economy), shows inevitable inconsistencies when
read in conjunction with the preface in which the changes that had taken place
in the intervening years were dealt with. There are several illustrations, and
those in colour based on paintings by Dora Ratman include a Parma cultivar
and two of John J. Kettle's semi-double cultivars; however, the remaining two,
entitled 'Sweet Violets of Every Hue' and 'A Representative Collection of
Present-Day Violets' lack keys to the cultivars depicted. This was a serious
omission as one can only make guesses, inspired or otherwise, as to the
various flowers' identities, a task made no easier by differences in the colours
of the inks used in the two editions: the artist's painstaking work has therefore
to some extent been wasted. Nevertheless, this is an excellent book, written by
one of the leading growers and whose nurseries were internationally famous.
It should be read by all present or intending violet growers.

—*Violets: Simple Hints on how to grow them* (Windward Violet Nurseries),
16pp.
In *Violets for Garden and Market,* Mrs Grace L. Zambra mentioned that

sales of this booklet, its forerunner, exceeded 10,000 copies. A general guide and list of cultivars offered for sale by her nurseries. Sections of this booklet entitled *Hints on Violet Growing* were sent out with plant orders until the nurseries closed down (temporarily) in 1963.

—'Winter Care of Violets' *Amateur Gardening*, 18 September 1958, p.5.

The Selected Catalog of the Library, compiled by Dorothy S. Manks (Massachusetts Horticultural Society, Boston, 1936) has been of use in preparing these notes.

Foreign Language Bibliography

Many articles by other writers have been published in Belgian, French and German periodicals. Violets have been grown on a large scale in many countries and contemporary national horticultural literature should reflect this popularity; a considerably under-researched subject awaits the horticultural historian.

Barandou, Pierre and others *Le Chant de la Violette* (Jardins de France, 1999).
Pierre Barandou, a French violet grower, provides a history of violet growing together with material on violet species and meristem propagation.

Bertrand, Bernard et Casbas, Nathalie *Une Pensee pour la Violette* (Editions de Terran, 2001)
An enthusiastic and wide-ranging account of various aspects of the violet and violet growing with numerous illustrations, including one of Dora Ratman's paintings.

Dauthenay, H. 'Violettes en Arbre', *Revue Horticole*, 16 March 1899.
Tree violets.

Millet, Armand *Les Violettes, leurs origines, leurs cultures* (Octave Doin et Libraire Agricole, 1898).
Essential reading for anyone researching the history of violet cultivation; the notes by E.J. Perfect to the English translation and also Edward A. Bunyard's comments on this book should also be studied.

Millet, Pere et Fils 'Les Violettes de nos Jours', *Le Jardin*, 20 March 1906.
One of many articles written jointly and separately by Armand Millet and his son, which were published in various French gardening periodicals, notably *Revue Horticole* and *Le Jardin*.

Mottet, S. 'Une Violette en Arbre', *Revue Horticole*, 1 June 1901.
Tree violets.

Nicholson, G. *Dictionaire Practique d'Horticulture et le Jardinage* (Libraire Agricole, 1899).

APPENDIX

RHS COLOUR REFERENCE CHART
Within the descriptive cultivar lists in this book there are references to the
Royal Horticultural Colour Chart. The object of the chart, prepared by the
Horticultural Society with the assistance and co-operation of the British
Colour Council, was to give a written code for the colour of a flower when
no colour image of the flower is provided. Yvonne Matthews has compared
blossoms typical of cultivars in the national collection of violets she holds
with the colour chart and has recorded the colour or range of colours that
appeared to be the nearest.

An example of the use of the colour chart numbers is given for 'Princess
Diana'. I have mentioned earlier in the book that there is some confusion
over the name, which I believe I have resolved. If the colour of the flowers is
approximately similar to chart colour 65D, the flower will be of the cultivar
originally listed under this name. If, however, the flower colour is in the range
58D to 62A it would be the sport known as 'Jean Arnot'. It is hoped that this
addition to the book along with another addition, colour illustrations, will
make the task of violet identification easier and help to reduce the number of
wrongly named stocks that are available.

The use of the colour chart numbers in this book is the first known attempt to
use the RHS colour chart in any book on violets. However, Beverley T.
Galloway did use colours from an older colour identification system in at
least one edition of his book *Commercial Violet Culture* in the early
twentieth century.

ABBREVIATIONS
The following abbreviations have been used:

AM	Award of Merit
CM	Certificate of Merit
FCC	First Class Certificate
FCHS	Central Horticultural Society (of France)
FNHS	The National Horticultural Society (of France)
RHS	Royal Horticultural Society
MRCF	Ministry Recommended Cut Flower where the cultivar was included in the Ministry of Agriculture series of advisory leaflets on Violets.

'Baron Rothschild' and 'Baronness (or Baronne) Rothschild'
I believe that the early flowering blue violet listed by both the Windward
Violet Nurseries and my nursery at Winchester as 'Baroness Rothschild' (or
'Baronne Alice de Rothschild') could actually have been 'Baron Rothschild'
with the later, purple-flowering violet being 'Baroness Rothschild'.

'Elsie Coombs'
I have been taken to task for referring to this cultivar as having an indigo
centre when it should in fact be Prussian blue (corrected in this edition). I
take the opportunity to stress that the cultivar is not a purple violet although
sometimes listed as such.

'George Lee's Violets and their Coding'
E. J. Perfect in his excellent article 'Russian Violets' in 1965, provided the
first account of George Lee's contribution to violet growing that had been
published for many years. The 1981 edition of this book provided additional
information and Jean Burrows, who rediscovered the violets still growing at
the former nursery on the terraced slopes of Tickenham Hill near Clevedon,
Somerset, has written about these events on several occasions (see Chapter 7
and Bibliography).

A selection of these rediscovered violets (the most distinct plants) were given
a code. The code consisted of firstly a capital letter, which was the first letter
of the surname of the owners of the particular part of the old nursery on
which that violet was found. The next part of the code was a running
number, one for each sequence found on that portion of the site, for example
H2 and H2a. All the selected plants were painstakingly recorded in
watercolour by Yvonne Matthews (illustrated in this book).

Subsequently the best of the selected plants were given names of Lee family
members by Jean Burrows, and for the closest to the original Clevedon violet,
the name 'Victoria Regina' was used. The named violets (and their former
codes) are 'Elizabeth Lee' (T3); 'Victoria Regina' (T4); 'George Lee' (T5);
'Florence Lee' (K6); 'Frances Lee' (K7); 'Theopolus Lee' (T61); 'Lee's Ivory'
(T62); Lee's Blue (T63); Lee's Peachy Pink (H23) and additionally there was a
purple violet with silver-edged foliage in the spring (H25).

The named plants now appear in nursery price lists and in pots awaiting sale.

SOCIETIES AND STOCKISTS

'As one engaged for years in its cultivation I have sometimes thought that it is worthy of a society of its own, as have the Rose, Carnation and Sweet Pea, to advocate its merits. But no, the Violet is both near and dear to the hearts of humanity. Could it speak I think it would shrink from notoriety. Its place is secure. No, it wants no society to press its claims'.

Frederick Dillistone, 1927

In 1980, when writing the first edition of this book, I thought that even if Dillistone had been right then, could the lack of a society for the violet be hampering its development now? I was certain that this was the case and I had already investigated the possibility of reviving the dormant London and South of England Viola Society with the idea of widening its activities to include violets. The revival of interest in violets and violet growing created a situation favourable to the launch of a society or other grouping of enthusiasts in the United Kingdom or abroad. The publication of the 1980 edition of the book proved a further catalyst. As such, two violet societies are now in existence.

The American Violet Society
www.americanvioletsociety.org
The American Violet Society is in the process of making more of its website available to the general public and other changes are taking place. It welcomes members from countries that have established violet-growing traditions, but also enthusiasts from other parts of the world.

The Violet Society
www.sweetviolets.com
Like the American Violet Society, it welcomes enthusiasts from all over the world.

VIOLET STOCKISTS

Bregover Plants, Hillbrooke, Middlewood, North Hill, Nr Launceston, Cornwall PL15 7NN, Tel 01566 782661

C. W. Groves and Son, The Nurseries, West Bay Road, Bridport, Dorset DT6 4BA , Tel 01308 422654
Groves and Son have extended the range of plants and other items for the gardener but the importance of the violet section of the business has increased dramatically. New cultivars have been raised and every possible attempt has been made to safeguard the older violets mentioned in this book.

Devon Violet Nursery, Rattery, South Brent, Devon TQ10 9LG, Tel 01364 643033
The development of this nursery has been even more dramatic. It has become the holder of the second of the UK's national violet collections.

Elizabeth MacGregor, Ellenbank, Tongland Road, Kirkcudbright, Dumfries and Galloway, Scotland DG6 4UU, Tel 01557 330620

Wisley Plant Centre, Wisley, Woking, Surrey GU23 6QB
This is perhaps of particular interest as a duplicate of my entire violet collection was donated to the RHS for conservation and trial purposes in the 1970s.

The Canyon Creek Nursery, 3527 Dry Creek Road, Oroville, CA 95965, USA
A grower of unusual garden plants. They have introduced new cultivars of violets as well as going to great lengths to safeguard the old. Details can be obtained from the nursery's website, www.canyoncreeknursery.com.

Logee's Greenhouses, 141 North Street, Danielson, Connecticut 06239, USA
Logee's Greenhouses has a long tradition of growing violets, which are listed as well as many other plants. Again there is a website: www.logees.com

Nathalie Casbas, Les Terres Blanches, 4 route de Villemur, 31620 Villaudric, France
Holder of the French national collection of old violet cultivars. An enthusiastic and knowledgable violet grower and writer.

Geraniums d'Acquitaine, 60, impasse de Péchabout, 47000 Agen, France
This is a long-established horticultural business that has developed an important violet section in comparatively recent years. Pierre Barandou, the head of the family, has contributed considerably to the literature of the violet.

Plants in Time, PO Box 1032, Ashwood Post Office, Ashwood 3147, Victoria, Australia
Plants in Time holds the Australian national collection of violets and has done much to conserve and distribute lesser-known violets partly via important overseas links.

CULTIVAR AND SPECIES INDEX

General Index